The secret rea[...]ork with
teens is their tu[...]ers to
a real world. That's what makes [...]le such a
gem—it comes from a heart that refuses to compro-
mise truth, and yet it is seasoned with the loving
tenderness of a father for his daughter.

I wholeheartedly recommend this book and have
copies tucked away until my own daughters begin that
thrilling, terrifying, and wondrous crossing into
adulthood.

—Bill Myers
author of McGee and Me! and Forbidden Doors series

Letters to Nicole are really letters to all of our teenage
sons and daughters. As a father of five teenagers myself,
I find Tim Smith's letters to his daughter, Nicole, full
of the kind of timely direction each of my kids wanted
and needed as they entered adolescence.

Tim minces no words and ducks no issues as he
speaks with a Christian father's heart and a seasoned
youth worker's wisdom. Parents will find *Letters to Nicole*
a valuable and one-of-a-kind tool for engaging their
teens in open discussion and reflection on the issues that
matter most to kids.

Parents who miss this book will look in vain to find
as comprehensive, biblical, and practical collection of
insights in a language kids can understand as Tim has
included in his *Letters to Nicole.*

—Kevin Huggins
author of *Parenting Adolescents*

Letters to Nicole is a must for any parent of an active teenage girl. It is a warm and loving presentation of godly wisdom. *Letters to Nicole* is filled with great ideas for surviving in a troubled and mixed-up world. The book carries the special emotions that are only felt between a father and his daughter.

I hope that the book will be a joy for the daughters who read it and the fathers who give it.

—Bob Phillips
author of *Good Clean Jokes for Kids*

Refreshing. Insightful. Creative. *Letters to Nicole* offers a wonderful gift to both parents and teens. This resource is honest, humorous, and fun. Tim Smith has outdone himself again.

—Dr. David Olshine
chairman of the Youth Ministries Department
Columbia International University
Columbia, South Carolina

Crammed with changes and challenges, the junior high years can be brutal for kids and their parents. In *Letters to Nicole,* Tim Smith provides help for both. Dealing with real-life problems, conflicts, and feelings, Tim communicates love, empathy, practical advice, and biblical wisdom to his daughter and to his readers. This book, or collection of letters as it might better be called, will be a valuable resource for moms and dads to read for insight and encouragement, to give to the early adolescent in the family, and to help bring parent and child together.

—Dave Veerman
senior editor of the *Life Application Bible for Students*
and author of *Parenting Passages*

Letters to Nicole

TIM SMITH

Tyndale House Publishers, Inc.

WHEATON, ILLINOIS

Other books by Tim Smith

Hi, I'm Bob and I'm the Parent of a Teenager—A Guide to Beginning and Leading a Support Group for Parents of Teens

8 Habits of an Effective Youth Worker

©1995 by Tim D. Smith
All rights reserved
Cover illustration copyright © 1995 by Sandra Speidel

All Scripture quotations, unless otherwise indicated, are taken from the *Holy Bible,* New International Version®. Copyright © 1973, 1978, 1984 by International Bible Society. Used by permission of Zondervan Publishing House. All rights reserved. The "NIV" and "New International Version" trademarks are registered in the United States Patent and Trademark Office by International Bible Society. Use of either trademark requires permission of International Bible Society.

Scripture verses marked TLB are taken from *The Living Bible,* copyright © 1971 owned by assignment by KNT Charitable Trust. All rights reserved.

Library of Congress Cataloging-in-Publication Data

Smith, Tim,   date
   Letters to Nicole / Tim Smith
      p.   cm.
   Includes indexes.
   Summary: Thirty letters from a father to his twelve-year-old daughter on such issues as expectations, self-esteem, emotions, sexuality, and spiritual growth.
   ISBN 0-8423-2046-6 (sc)
   1. Fathers and daughters—Juvenile literature.   [1. Fathers and daughters.   2. Conduct of life.   3. Christian life.]   I. Title.
HQ777.S63   1995
306.874'2—dc20   95-16422

Printed in the United States of America

01   00   99   98   97   96   95
 7   6   5   4   3   2   1

*"To have a daughter
is to know a special kind of joy."*

Dedicated to our daughter
Nicole Noel Smith

May you continue to be a
"Victorious Heart"

CONTENTS

Dear Reader:

Forewords are usually a bore, aren't they? But now and then, they ring our must-buy bell, and we are hooked. That's what I'd like to do right now.

Nicole is a new teenager, and so are thousands of others like her. So I have some questions for you. Do you have a Nicole on your heart who needs your special love right now? A daughter? granddaughter? neighbor? Someone on your friendship list? A new teenager in your church family?

Whoever she is, can you look deep enough inside her to see the emotional goings-on? Whether you like it or not, she's excited at all these possibilities. But she's confused, too. New friends calling her over here, over there: "Oh, come on. You're a big girl now. Live a little. Everybody does it." Do they? How important are the *yes*es and *no*s she's been hearing? Who can she believe out here on her own? "Oh, God, please help me. Can't I turn and run back again to six or nine? Maybe eleven? It's scary out here. Am I really ready to know what to let go and when to say no?"

You'll be praying for her, won't you? Of course you will. You've always prayed for her. But here's the point of my letter: *Have you provided her mind with adequate data for thinking ahead? Have you equipped her with wise and loving advice for these scary years she's facing?*

If you're even a bit unsure of your answer, *Letters to Nicole* is your book. Tim Smith offers us here a love treasure for gift giving. A precious gift for the budding teen. So here's that question again: Parent, grandparent, friend, teacher—is there a girl in your caring circle who needs you right now? There she goes, off into a world of teen confusion, bewilderment, right choices or wrong. I know from experience how one book can guide and bless where the Lord needs it. But books need friends, too; friends who care enough for others to share their love.

It is my prayer that *Letters to Nicole* will sell and sell, to bless and bless.

Love,
Charlie Shedd

Editor's Note: Charlie Shedd is the author of *Letters to Karen* and *Letters to Philip*, which have sold over 10 million copies since their publication nearly thirty years ago. His most recent book is *Brush of an Angel's Wing*.

These letters are my words. But the ideas and values I share with my wife, Suzanne. I am grateful for her contribution to this book, our family, and my life.

ONE

The Pressure of Expectations

A diamond is a chunk of coal that
is made good under pressure.

—DAD

Dear Nicole,

Today, when you exploded after school, I wanted to hug you
and erase the pressure of the day. I remember the tears in your
eyes when you asked, "Everyone wants more than I can give.
Why do I feel so pressured?"

You've had a hard day. Your teachers have piled on homework, some of your friends were grouchy but expected you to
be understanding. You also blew that test.

Now you're home, and you turn on the television and col-
lapse. Immediately you're bombarded with advertisements
that tell you unless you use their toothpaste, you won't get the
guy.

Then Mom says, "Clean up the dog messes!" and that is the
last straw! You explode and are sent to your room.

What can you do? How can you handle the pressure? First,
it might help to look at where the pressure comes from. Think
back over the day just described.

In elementary school you had one teacher; now you have
six. Each teacher thinks his subject and his assignments are the
most important. Each one expects you to complete all the
requirements of his class.

Friends also place expectations on you. That's just the
nature of friendship. It is a relationship of give and take, but
too often there is more take than give.

Nicole, think back to the test. You were disappointed with

1

your grade because you'd expected to do better. Can you see that you also make demands on yourself? When you don't measure up to your own expectations, you become discouraged.

As your dad and mom, we have expectations too. We expect you to do certain things and have a right attitude when you do them. We expect you to be learning responsibility.

The world you live in also expects you to look and act a certain way. If you don't, you will not be accepted. Nicole, do you ever wish you were a little kid again? In fact, that's part of the problem—the world you grew up in would never really let you be a child. Your little baby clothes copied grown-up clothes, and your toys copied the grown-up world. You've always been pressured to do better and be more grown-up!

So what can you do to cope? Realize that some expectations are valid and others are not. Nicole, you don't have to buy the toothpaste or look and act like the world tells you. When you mess up, learn all you can from it and move on.

When Jesus lived on earth he was surrounded by people making demands on him, yet he never seemed pressured. He was always looking to God to help him. He understands the pressure you're feeling today, and he will help you through it. Listen to what he said:

> *Come to me, all you who are weary and*
> *burdened, and I will give you rest.*
> MATTHEW 11:28

It is my prayer that you will get a break from the pressure you are facing.

Love,

Dad

What do you think?

When did you feel pressure today?

_____

_____

_____

_____

Riding the Emotional Roller Coaster

He leads me beside quiet waters.

—PSALM 23:2

Dear Nicole,

I've noticed you've been real excited and real disappointed within minutes of each other. My guess is you are wondering how to ride this roller coaster of emotions. Have you recently asked yourself, "How can I handle the ups and downs of my emotions?"

Let me see if I can help. Imagine with me. . . . You have been looking forward to the party, your calendar has been marked for weeks, and you know exactly what you're going to wear. The day finally arrives, and you join your friends, excited and happy. Yet, less than an hour later you hit rock bottom. You're angry and depressed, and you feel like an isolated island in a sea of happy, confident faces. You may feel you can't even bring your emotions up to the point where you can act normal.

What happened? How did you go from high to low so fast? Any number of things may have made you feel out of place or unwanted. Someone may have laughed at you, or someone you cared about may have ignored you.

Why do you have these uncontrollable swings in your feelings? Think back to the party. Something happened to trigger your emotions—something changed. That is the key. Change! Nicole, everything is changing in your life right now.

Your body is changing, and physical changes affect the emotions.

Your lifestyle is changing. From seventh grade on, you leave the relative security of one teacher and a roomful of kids for six different classes, with different teachers and classmates in each one. Talk about stress! You have to find your place in each of these classes and make new friends. Don't forget that every other kid is coping with the same emotional ups and downs as you are. This makes for amazing complications in your relationships with one another.

How can you handle this roller-coaster ride of emotions? First, accept the fact that you will be on a roller coaster for a while. Realize that what you are experiencing is perfectly normal and temporary. Learn this little phrase and repeat it to yourself often: "This, too, shall pass." Then, hang on for the ride! Picture a roller coaster as it creeps slowly up the almost vertical tracks, reaches the top, and seems poised there for a few seconds. Suddenly—with a jerk—it is flying downward! That may describe your emotions in a nutshell.

You try to climb out of the pit, and it is a hard, uphill effort. Then you look around and see that you are making progress, feeling a little better. You strain for the top, to feel good about yourself, and then something happens—you get a bad grade or have a fight with a friend—and you feel the familiar jerk that plummets you down again.

All this is tiring and confusing. Emotions can affect your ability to concentrate in school, to get your chores done at home, and even to sleep. Thoughts and emotions fill you so completely that you are distracted and irritable. You don't want anyone to bug you—not your teachers, your family, or even, at times, your friends. When you go to bed everything races through your mind so you cannot sleep.

Nicole, all your emotions are magnified, bigger than life right now. Think about it this way: When you first learned how to write, remember how big the spaces were between the lines on your paper? Remember how sloppy your writing was? No matter how big the spaces were, you still could not stay within the lines. Then as you practiced and the muscles in your hands grew more coordinated, your writing became more even. Each year, as the spaces became smaller, you learned to stay within the lines.

The same is true with your emotions. Nicole, you are just beginning to really experience them, and they won't stay within the lines! But God built you and your emotions to work together. As you grow and develop, they will become more even. In time, they will balance.

Dear Daughter, this is a hard time in your life, but it is not impossible. You are about to emerge into the person God wants you to be, so hang on for the ride!

The good news is, where there is a roller coaster—there is cotton candy!

Love,
Dad

What do you think?

Besides a roller coaster, what illustration describes your emotions? (Example: "I feel like a dragster, full race—then stop.")

_____

_____

_____

_____

_____

Putting a Leash on Your Temper

A fight is an argument that ran out of words.

—DAD

Dear Nicole,

I hate to admit it, but I also struggle with my temper. I guess you are a chip off the old block—sorry about that.

If you are like me, sometimes you're surprised when you blow up. You wonder, *Where did that come from?*

Nicole, can you think of a time when you got really ticked and said or did things that you felt sorry for later? I can.

It's kind of scary wondering why we lose control and let our temper take over. It's important to remember that when we get angry it often is because things aren't going as we had planned.

One way that helps me control my temper is not to expect that things will always go *just* the way I want them to. Instead of expecting my day to go perfectly, I try to allow for some detours, surprises, and interruptions. This is called "being flexible." If we can be flexible, we can still have a pretty good day even when unpleasant surprises come along, and not let our temper ruin it.

Another reason we lose our temper is that we get hurt. People say things or do things that cause us pain. Anger is a natural response to being hurt.

> *"In your anger do not sin." Do not let the sun*
> *go down while you are still angry.*
> EPHESIANS 4:26

9

Nicole, you can see from this verse that we can be angry and still not sin. It's not wrong to *be* angry, but what we *do* with our anger can be either right or wrong. If someone does something that hurts you, it's OK to be angry—*but* be careful what you say or do until you cool down.

Let's say you are in line for lunch and someone cuts in front of you, knocking over your drink. It's not wrong to be mad at that person's selfishness, but it would be wrong for you to cuss them out or hit them over the head with your tray of food (even though that would be tempting!).

Usually what gets us in trouble is not the anger itself, but *reacting* in anger. Controlling your temper is like driving a car. You are controlling something that can be very helpful or very destructive. When you drive a car and come to the railroad tracks, what are you supposed to do? That's right: *stop, look, and listen.*

Nicole, the same thing is true with your temper. The next time you are tempted to lose your temper, *stop*—don't react in anger. *Look*—see what caused your anger; see if you are partly at fault. *Listen*—ask yourself a few questions, like "Is this worth fighting for?" And ask the person you are mad at questions like "Can you tell me why you did that?" They used to say, "Count to ten before you get angry." This is what you can do while you are counting:

Take note of this: Everyone should be quick to listen, slow to speak and slow to become angry, for man's anger does not bring about the righteous life that God desires.
JAMES 1:19-20

Watching the sunset,

Dad

What do you think?

Complete the following sentence: "I really hate it
when . . ."

_____

_____

_____

_____

_____

Words Will Never Hurt Me

FOUR

*Every day our words impact others—they
either build them up or tear them down.*

—DAD

Dear Nicole,

I know you are hurting because of the mean things the "popular kids" said to you. I wanted to write to let you know I understand how you feel.

Rejection is a painful thing. The word *reject* means "to refuse to recognize or accept, to discard as worthless." That's just how you feel when you have been rejected, right? Unacceptable, unrecognized, unworthy. You want to say, "Hey, wait a minute! I'm here, I count for something!" So how do you handle it?

The first thing to realize is that sometimes you *think* you are being rejected when you are not. For instance, it's lunch-time and you leave your group to go get something from the snack bar. The line moves slowly, and by the time you get back your friends have disappeared. You're hurt! And mad! How could they leave you? Where did they go, and what are you supposed to do, standing there like a fool, hands loaded with food? You feel you are not worth much if they couldn't even wait for you to get back. It's understandable that you'd be hurt. But what really happened is that someone forgot an assignment for next period and they all went back to her locker to get it. They did not purposely reject you. When that kind of thing happens, try to be understanding and forgiving.

Nicole, sometimes you may feel rejected by our family when all the attention goes to your sister. At times, you may feel that everyone seems to make a fuss over her and exclude you. Your emotions get in an uproar, and once again you're mad! And hurt!

Stop and think for a minute. Is there a reason for all this attention? Did she bring her grades up or do well at gymnastics? You may feel that we're rejecting *you,* but actually it's just *her* moment to shine!

Then, sometimes, rejection is very real. When a friend rejects you, that really hurts! You feel discarded and worthless. The only way to handle it is to remember that no matter what your friend thinks, you *are* acceptable; you *do* have worth.

Think about the food you hate the most in the entire world. For you, that may be lima beans! Don't you reject them with disgust? Sure, but other people love lima beans! I do!

Nicole, that's how it is with people, too. Maybe someone has turned their back on you (the way you reject lima beans), but there are others who still like you and think highly of you (the way I like lima beans). Hang on to that! Also hang on to the fact that God will never reject you. His love for you never fails, and he believes in who you are and what you will become. A verse that has helped me when I feel rejected and lonely is Hebrews 13:5-6:

God has said, "Never will I leave you; never will I forsake you." So we say with confidence, "The Lord is my helper; I will not be afraid. What can man do to me?"

By the way, I'll always love you. I'll *never* reject you.

Love forever,

Dad

What do you think?

What is it about rejection that makes it so scary?

_____

_____

_____

_____

_____

Masterpiece in the Mirror

True beauty shines from a heart at peace.

—DAD

Dear Nicole,

Today when you said, "I don't like the way I look. Why did God make me like this?" I wasn't sure what to say. Since then I've given it some thought, and here are a few of my ideas.

I know you will not believe this, but God made you the way you are because he wanted you to be like him! Each one of us is "made in his image," the Bible says. When God was creating this world and he decided to make people, he said, "Let us make man in our image, in our likeness" (Genesis 1:26). Nicole, being made in God's image is what sets you apart from a tree or a dog. It means you have the ability to think and to make decisions about right and wrong. You have emotions and are able to communicate. You also have creative abilities (which trees and dogs don't!).

There are over four billion people in this world, and every one of them was created in God's image. You . . . me . . . your sister . . . and even the worst criminal you have ever heard of! At the same time, every single person in this world is different and unique. Nicole, you are unique. There is no one else in the world who is like you! There never has been since the beginning of time, and there never will be for eternity.

God is like an artist who never runs out of ideas when he is forming human beings. He doesn't have to make any copies. Each person is a carefully crafted masterpiece.

You created my inmost being; you knit
me together in my mother's womb.
PSALM 139:13

Do you realize that God crafted you before you were born?
He carefully designed each part of you.

Nicole, can you remember as a kid how you felt when you
made something all by yourself? You felt proud and satisfied,
like you had really accomplished something good. Remember
what happened when you showed it to somebody else and you
could tell they didn't think it was too great? You felt discouraged and let down.

We do the same thing to God when we don't like the way
he made us. Every time you look in the mirror and say, "I hate
my hair," or "I can't stand the color of my eyes," or "I hate the
way I'm built," you tell God you can't stand his creation.

My dear daughter, here is a practical thing to do: Copy this
verse and tape it up on your mirror.

I praise you because I am fearfully and wonderfully made; your
works are wonderful, I know that full well.
PSALM 139:14

Nicole, thank God for the way he has made you. I know this
is asking a lot, but if you will do this, you will find yourself,
little by little, growing free of your worry about how you look.
Give it a try!

By the way, I think you're beautiful.

Dad

What do you think?

Why do some people have a difficult time accepting how they look?

_____

_____

_____

_____

_____

Testing the Waters of Lake Grown-Up

SIX

When I was a child, I talked like a child, I thought like a child,
I reasoned like a child. When I became a man,
I put childish ways behind me.

—1 CORINTHIANS 13:11

Dear Nicole,

You're caught in the middle between being a child and being an adult. It's a tough spot to be in. I'm sure that at times you aren't sure how to act. This is a confusing time in your life, with one foot in the adult world and the other still in the world of childhood.

You know what it's like to stand at the edge of a lake? You want to go in, but you know the water is going to be cold. So you stick just your toes in, then quickly pull your foot back out. You were right! It *is* too cold to go in. You inch back onto the warm shore until you get up the nerve to try it again.

That's how it is with your life right now. The child's world is warm and secure because you know it so well. The adult world is cold, and although you want to step out into it, it's big and scary. Sometimes you dip your toes in, but every time you venture there, you are expected to respond in new ways to new situations. The water is too cold, so you beat a hasty retreat to dry ground, acting like a child again.

For instance, one week you handle your chores around the house with admirable maturity. You have no problem making your bed each day, keeping your room straightened, and picking up after Bingo. The next week, however, everything in you rebels. You act just like when you were little and you used to stamp your foot and say, "No!"

21

Or perhaps you are with a group of friends, and you feel mature, capable of handling anything. You're saying the right things and acting the right way. Then all of a sudden you start to act silly and childish. How stupid you feel, but you can't seem to help yourself!

Little by little, however, the grown-up world will become more familiar to you, just like the cold lake feels warmer as your body becomes used to it. Soon you'll be swimming through the water and enjoying it. Nicole, as you become more used to new areas of growth and maturity, it will become easier to let go of your child's world.

No hurry, though. Take your time. Too many kids rush to grow up.

Dad

What do you think?

Think of a time when you weren't sure whether you were supposed to act like a kid or an adult. What did you do? How did you feel?

_____

_____

_____

_____

_____

Bad Days

SEVEN

*It's one thing to try and fail, and
another thing to fail to try.*

—Dad

Dear Nicole,

Today started out bad for you and only got worse! You had to
give an oral report first period, and you're sure you did an
awful job. You walked up to a group during break time, started
to say something, and they looked at you as if you had just
landed from Mars. Was it your outfit? It was the third one you
put on this morning! Was it something you said? Why can't you
ever feel confident and secure with what you are saying, or
doing, or wearing? You still have to face P.E., and that ties your
stomach in knots of worry. The thought of others seeing you in
your P.E. clothes is almost more than you can bear. When you
have to do tests in P.E., your body acts like none of its parts are
related!

Nicole, we all have days like this—when we are painfully
aware of everything we do and say and wonder what others are
thinking about us. This is called feeling self-conscious. What we
often fail to realize is that others aren't usually paying that
much attention to us. They are far too busy worrying about
how *they* look to *us!*

At times like these it seems the harder you try, the worse
things get. But actually you're not blowing it at all—you're
just blowing it out of proportion. Elijah, one of God's proph-
ets, had a similar experience.

Elijah was running away from an evil queen, Jezebel, who
was trying to kill him. "I have had enough, Lord," he said. "I

23

am the only one left [on God's side], and now they are trying to kill me too!" God told Elijah he was blowing this out of proportion. He told him to get up and try again, and (by the way) there were still seven thousand faithful people in Israel. (This is all in 1 Kings 19.)

It's easy to blow things out of proportion when you have your eyes on yourself and your circumstances. That's what happened to Elijah. That is what happens to us.

Nicole, here are some ideas to help you get through days like these. First, understand that you may not be seeing yourself clearly. It's as if you are going through a house of mirrors at a carnival. You see yourself a dozen different ways, but they're all distorted. They don't reflect the real you. Once you are home, standing before your own mirror, you see a clear reflection. You have to get away from the distorted mirrors.

Second, remember that everyone else is just as concerned with themselves as you are. They probably aren't even noticing you because they are preoccupied with themselves.

Third, keep in mind God's picture of you. He has a portrait of you as a mature, godly young woman. He'll help you as you grow to match that picture.

For the Lord will be your confidence and
will keep your foot from being snared.
PROVERBS 3:26

Your fellow struggler,
Dad

What do you think?

When is it easy for you to blow things out of proportion and feel defeated?

_____

_____

_____

_____

_____

EIGHT

When You Feel Shy

Don't waste your words on fools.

—DAD

Dear Nicole,

I know you are facing some new situations that make you uncomfortable. While you're usually confident and outgoing, some of these situations have forced you to be on your own, and you've discovered yourself "being shy."

For instance . . . that party you went to where you stood at the door and looked in. How you dreaded having to enter that room! *Who will I talk to? What will I say?* You just knew you would stumble over all your words and feel like a fool. *What's wrong with me? Why can't I just walk up to someone, start talking, and say the right thing?*

When you have to break into a group, do you feel like you're the only one struggling? Does it seem like a great big spotlight is focused on you? Everyone else seems self-assured, while you are in agony.

Actually, most of the other kids in the room feel as unsure as you do, but we all mask our insecurities.

Nicole, it's OK to feel unsure of yourself at this point in your life. You are facing lots of new situations. It's natural to proceed slowly, like you would if you were hiking down a steep mountain trail. Feel your way cautiously so you won't fall flat on your face!

Sometimes it's appropriate to be quiet. It helps us tune in and listen. I think we can learn a lot in situations like that. In new situations, we probably need the information we can get by being quiet rather than by talking a whole bunch.

The Bible tells of two sisters, Martha and Mary. Martha was definitely not shy! When Jesus was a guest in her house, she complained to him about her sister. "Lord, don't you care that my sister has left me to do the work by myself? Tell her to help me!" Now Mary had been sitting with Jesus, listening to everything he said. Jesus' response was, "Mary has chosen what is better" (Luke 10:40, 42). Jesus affirms the value of a quiet, listening attitude!

Israel's great leader, Moses, was very unsure of himself. God came to him in the desert and told him to go back to Egypt and rescue his people from slavery. Moses thought of every excuse in the book! "But I'm not the person for a job like that!" he exclaimed. *I'm too insignificant for God to use,* he probably thought. Then he said, "They won't believe me! They won't do what *I* tell them to." His last excuse was, "O Lord, I'm just not a good speaker. I never have been, and I'm not now, even after you have spoken to me, for I have a speech impediment" (Exodus 3:11; 4:1, 10, TLB).

Each time, God reassured him and took care of his insecurities. Moses became a powerful leader, and God used him in a mighty way in spite of his shyness.

Moses stepped out in faith, but I'm sure when he reached Egypt he felt much like you did, Nicole, when you stood at that door! *Who do I talk to and what do I say?* If you find yourself without the confidence or the words (like Moses), ask God for a little backup. I find myself doing this all the time. Yeah, I know, hard to believe—but it's true.

Mouthfully yours,

Dad

What do you think?

What are some good things about feeling shy?

_____

_____

_____

_____

_____

Escape Routes from Temptation

NINE

I have kept my feet from every evil path
so that I might obey your word.
—PSALM 119:101

Dear Nicole,

I noticed some guys at your school staring at the girls and making nasty comments. They were showing that they were trapped by lust and had lost self-control. I didn't like what I saw, but I understood it.

The other day I was standing in front of a donut shop. The donuts looked so inviting, as if they were saying to me, "We are lonely. Come eat us! Don't leave us in this glass cage!"

I took a closer look to see if they really did look like they needed a companion, someone to hold them and enjoy their sweetness. As I took that second look, I felt my feet following the scent that gently wafted out the door like jasmine on the morning ocean breeze. It had me captivated. . . . I was going in. I had lost control.

Earlier that week I had walked by that shop several times and resisted the urge to go in and buy a donut. I was trying to stay off sweets, and donuts were a real temptation for me. Why had I yielded to temptation? Why couldn't I just look and keep on walking?

I think I gave in because I had overloaded my temptation defense mechanism. You see, each of us has the ability to resist temptation, but sometimes we overload this ability and it does not work. It's not wrong to be tempted. We are all tempted. The problem comes when we give in to temptation.

Nicole, can you think of something in your life that shows

that you are losing the battle with temptation? Chances are, you can. Let's think about some of the things that make it hard to resist temptation.

One of the first things I think about is being in the wrong place. There are certain places where it is too easy to give in to temptation, such as places where other people are giving in to the temptation that you are trying to resist.

For instance, many times young teens go to parties where people drink beer or some kind of alcohol. If you are tempted to drink but don't want to, it's stupid to go to parties where drinking is going on. It's like saying you don't want to eat donuts, but walking past the shop every day. If you want to have victory over a certain temptation, you may have to *avoid certain places.*

Another thing you'll need to do to beat temptation is to *avoid being with the wrong people.* In junior high, I couldn't figure out why I had a chair in the principal's office with my name on it. You see, two of my friends were always getting into trouble. I was with them, so I got in trouble too. One day, as I sat in Mr. Baldwin's office, it hit me: *If I just don't hang around with these guys, I won't get in trouble!* Brilliant, huh?

It was Joseph, a guy in the Old Testament, who taught me the third way to avoid temptation's snare: *Be ready to run when it gets too hot.* You may remember the story—Joseph was working for Potiphar and really doing a great job. He received all kinds of promotions and honors. Potiphar really liked him. (This story is in Genesis 39.)

One day, Mrs. Potiphar noticed that Joseph was a pretty good-looking dude. She tried to seduce him, but he saw what was happening, so he literally ran away from her, leaving his coat in her hot little hands.

Joseph had learned that there are times when temptation is so strong that we should not hang around to discuss it or think about it. Sometimes it's best to run now and think later.

A fourth tip on avoiding temptation is *be alert and ready for sneak attacks.*

Be self-controlled and alert. Your enemy the devil prowls around like a roaring lion looking for someone to devour. Resist him, standing firm in the faith.
1 PETER 5:8-9

The devil is sneaky, and he wants to destroy your life. But he doesn't send you a fax that reads, "I'm planning on attacking you tomorrow night at the movies." The devil wants to surprise you with a sneak attack. He won't give you a warning.

We stay alert by expecting the devil to attack us in our weak spots. For example, I know I'm weakest when I'm tired, hungry, or hurt, so those are times I need to be especially alert to temptation. If we can stay alert, we can be prepared to resist temptation—the kind that comes from inside us and the kind that comes from outside us.

The fifth tip on escaping the magnetic pull of temptation is *memorize Scripture and use it to defeat temptation.* The Bible can be like a pocket knife that you can pull out and use to cut yourself free from the vines that tangle you up and pull you into temptation.

I run in the path of your commands,
for you have set my heart free.
PSALM 119:32

Nicole, I like this verse because it teaches us that true freedom comes from obeying God's commands. When we "run in the path" of God's commands, we stay free from the temptations that try to control us. Our heart can be free from guilt because we did not give in to temptation. We can be free!

Temptation doesn't always have to win. God has promised to help us right in the middle of the temptation. One way God helps us is by giving us strength from his Word. Daughter, memorize this promise, and recite it out loud next time you are tempted. It tells us that God won't let any temptation come into our life that we can't handle.

No temptation has seized you except what is common to man. And God is faithful; he will not let you be tempted beyond what you can bear. But when you are tempted, he will also provide a way out so that you can stand up under it.
1 CORINTHIANS 10:13

I learned this verse as a teenager, and I have used it so much that I thought I would wear it out. But you can't wear out God's promises; they work forever.

Nicole, your name means "victorious heart." I pray that you will be victorious over temptation.

With you in the battle,
Dad

What do you think?

What has helped you escape temptation?

_____

_____

_____

_____

_____

Tanya's Big Question

To live a life that is distinctive,
be committed to purity.

—DAD

Dear Nicole,

Years ago, one of the girls in the youth group asked me a very important question. Tanya had a boyfriend and needed help.

"I really like him," she started, "and I want to be able to show him I care—plus he's such a hunk. Why can't I express myself to him? How far can I go and still not be sinning?"

I knew Tanya well enough to know that she was very serious about this question and it demanded a careful answer. I gave her the following illustration. We talked about you!

"Tanya, you know Nicole. She loves to ride her bike in front of our house. She knows that she is not to ride out in the middle of the street or more than four houses down the block in either direction. [I told you this was years ago!]

"Another rule is that she is not to go out there unless her mom or I know about it or are outside with her. Does this sound cruel and mean? No, it is a way of protecting her. We love our daughter and have rules to protect her from harm. The rules aren't bad, the world is.

"Some people say the world is good and the rules are bad, but the opposite is true. The world is an evil place, and we can get hurt if we don't follow God's rules."

"So what does God say—no kissing and hugging? Or does he say anything at all?" Tanya asked. Tanya wouldn't settle for easy answers!

"Well," I responded, stalling to try to think up something.

"God doesn't come right out and spell out the specifics, but he does give us some principles as guidelines."

"What are they? And don't tell me no kissing until marriage," Tanya insisted.

Here is what I told her: "God made sex for marriage. Listen to this verse:

> *Marriage should be honored by all, and the marriage*
> *bed kept pure, for God will judge the adulterer*
> *and all the sexually immoral.*
> HEBREWS 13:4

"So obviously sex before marriage is a definite no-no. But what about all the other things, other than sexual intercourse? God will judge those who sin sexually. He does not want us to be impure. The big question is, where do you draw the line? I think it has a lot to do with the individual."

"I agree," Tanya said, nodding. "Some guys I know can't even hold your hand without having major hormone problems!"

We laughed, and I continued. "The Bible emphasizes purity, not any specific physical act. For some people, holding hands is the limit, because anything more would cause them to lust (want each other sexually). In other words, what goes on in your mind is just as important as what your hands do. One Scripture that helps us get this idea of purity is:

> *Don't let anyone look down on you because you are young,*
> *but set an example for the believers in speech, in life,*
> *in love, in faith and in purity.*
> 1 TIMOTHY 4:12

"So it's not just one thing—the whole lifestyle matters. You don't want to do anything or say anything that might cause people to doubt that you are a believer. In other words, if most of the girls at your school are making out with their boyfriends and you do the exact same thing, they won't know the difference between you and those who don't believe in Jesus. There should be some kind of difference. Christians need to have an observably higher standard."

"Do I have to be weird about it? How do I set and keep higher standards?" asked Tanya.

"Your friends need to see your commitment to purity. It's a total commitment. Not just what you don't do (or do), but who you *are*. If they can see your commitment to purity, it will provide an example for them. Too many kids don't have standards. They let everyone else tell them what's right. That's not leading, that's following. Last I checked, there are plenty of followers, but a shortage of leaders. God wants us to be this kind of leader in our relationships with the opposite sex. He wants us to be examples of purity."

I wasn't sure if I had done a good job of explaining this to Tanya, so I asked her, "How far do you think you can go and still keep your purity?"

She responded with an intelligent answer. *"Not far!* But you should consider how old the people are, how long they have gone with each other, and how much self-control they have. It will take a lot of self-control to stay pure."

"Wow, that's great," I commended her. "You've really thought this topic through. Remember, Tanya, the goal isn't really to see how close you can get to the edge of the cliff, but to learn how you can protect something precious—your purity—and to honor God in all that you do."

"Yeah, I know. But are there *any* specific guidelines you can give me?"

"Well, OK, here are a few ideas to start with." And here's basically what I told her:

1. Hand-holding and sitting close to each other can be

great ways to enjoy each other without getting your-
selves into a bad situation.

2. Kissing on the first date is foolish, and kisses that take a
   long time will just get you into trouble. Remember,
   kisses are not a repayment for a hamburger and a movie.

3. Don't lie down beside each other, especially if all you
   have on are your swimsuits. The temptation is just too
   strong.

4. Caressing or touching each other on the breasts and in
   the genital area is one guaranteed way to lose control.
   Never do this.

5. Don't be alone with your date in his home when his
   parents aren't there. No sitting on laps and no sitting
   together in a parked car. These are situations where
   your impulses can drive you much farther than your
   godly intentions.

Nicole, a girl takes a boy's physical attention as proof that he
really cares for her. The boy may have "caring for her" very far
down his list of reasons for touching her more and more inti-
mately. The surprise for the young woman with godly intentions
is that, in spite of knowing that she shouldn't be letting him do
what he's doing, she likes it! She pushes down the nagging
twinge of guilt because she didn't know these new feelings
would be so positive.

Tanya is now married to a handsome, loving, Christian man.
She was able to keep her purity for him. I saw her a while ago
and she exclaimed, "Thanks for the sex advice, it really works!"
She said it loudly so people around could hear. I was embar-
rassed, but more than that, I was proud. Tanya always had a
way of making difficult topics fun. You remind me of her.

Proudly,

Dad

What do you think?

Tanya was given a lot of advice. Which piece of advice seems to be the best for you?

_____

_____

_____

_____

_____

ELEVEN

Swimming with Sharks

Loitering with losers is like
swimming with sharks.

—DAD

Dear Nicole,

If I had a dollar for every time I've been asked "Should I date a non-Christian?" I'd be able to buy you a car for your sixteenth birthday!

Lisa was an attractive fifteen-year-old who looked like she was seventeen. One day she asked me, "Tim, do you think it's OK for me to date a non-Christian if we don't get too serious?"

"What's this guy like?" I asked.

"Oh, he's considerate, cool, and good-looking. My parents even like him!" she exclaimed.

"Lisa, the question isn't really whether you should date a non-Christian, but whether you're ready to date," I explained.

"How do I know if I'm ready?" asked Lisa.

Here's what I told her: "A person is ready to date when they know the benefits and dangers of dating and they have written out their personal dating standards. When you are aware of the benefits and dangers of dating and can describe them, you'll be much more aware of what to pursue or avoid in your dating relationships.

"Dating can be dangerous! Whenever you're getting ready to do something that involves potential danger, you prepare for it. Not preparing for dating is like going skydiving without learning how. It hurts too much to learn by trial and error!"

Lisa smiled and said, "I think I know the benefits and dangers, but what is this idea about standards?"

41

"Think about playing soccer. You can't really play unless you know the rules and the point of the game and have some kind of strategy. Dating standards help you figure out how you're going to play the game and what rules you're going to stick to."

Nicole, one of your dating standards could include what kind of person you'll date—how much older, younger, or different from you. My suggestion is not to start dating one-on-one the first year you date. Go to events with a group of friends or double-date. Group dates take a lot of pressure off you and help you get to know what kind of guys you like.

Dating a non-Christian isn't a sin, but it can lead to one. The Bible warns us not to be "yoked together with unbelievers. For what do righteousness and wickedness have in common?" (2 Corinthians 6:14).

A person is "yoked" with another person when they have made a commitment to be together and not to go out with others. I'm not sure if "going steady" is the same as "being yoked," but I'm sure you get the point.

Nicole, God doesn't want us to have long-term romantic relationships with people who don't know him. Why? Because they have different values and priorities, and that will create all kinds of conflict in the relationship.

Dating a person a few times to get to know him and find out if he is a Christian may be OK. But don't play games, kidding yourself that "sooner or later I'll talk to him about the Lord."

Here is one suggestion for how to handle your first few dates with someone. On the first date you'll want to get to know your date, his personality, and what kinds of things he likes.

On the second date you'll talk to him about what's important to each of you. You can discuss values and your family backgrounds.

If it hasn't come up yet, then on the third date you'll tell your friend what is *really* important to you—that is, your relationship with Jesus. Ask him what he thinks about what you said, and ask him about his beliefs. If he is not a Christian, ask if he's interested in finding out more about Christ by going to a Christian activity with you. If he is a Christian, consider whether you want to go out a fourth time.

Nicole, with this strategy you can find out fairly quickly where a guy is in his relationship with God. It also helps keep you from rushing into a relationship with an unbeliever.

If your date isn't a believer or isn't willing to go with you to church or Christian activities, he will negatively affect your faith. It's harmful to get involved with someone who has a different focus in life.

Another problem is going out with a stagnant Christian— one who isn't growing. Many teenage girls have told me this kind is the worst. "They know the Christian words, but practically attack you when you're alone."

Make sure you are sharing your heart with someone who values what's in it.

Cautiously caring,

Dad

What do you think?

What do you think are some of the benefits and dangers of dating?

_____

_____

_____

_____

_____

The Why behind the No

TWELVE

*Teens often mistake sex for love
and fondling for affection.*

—DAD

Dear Nicole,

I know teens. I talk to them every day. Sooner or later you'll
be joining them in asking yourself, *Why should I remain a virgin?
No one else is!*

"She's probably the last virgin in Los Angeles!"

"Ha ha ha hee hee!" went the laughs in the theater. It was the
movie *Dragnet,* and the virgin was about to be sacrificed by the
bad guys. Every person in the theater laughed at the joke.

What about that fourteen-year-old girl sitting in front of me? I
thought. *Will she decide that it is "uncool" to be a virgin?* The movie
treated virginity like a disease—something to get rid of.

This kind of mythmaking makes me very sad. Nicole, you are
not weird or childish just because you haven't had sex. You are a
valuable person, even though you are "uneducated" sexually.

You probably have noticed that your body will send you signals sometimes that say, *Wow! His body needs to get next to mine!*
You find yourself attracted to guys. This is good. God made
you that way. Your body will get excited and tell you to "go for
it!" But your body will not tell you how having sex now may
harm you.

Did you know that over one million teenage girls become
pregnant each year? AIDS and other sexually transmitted diseases are at epidemic levels—and some have no cure. Most
cause incredible pain, some cause sterility, and some cause
death.

Why do people think sex is such a big thing? It seems that having sex makes many teens feel like they are mature; others do it to be popular or to be part of the "in" crowd. Some teens feel that everyone is doing it, and they don't want to be left out. (Nicole, don't be fooled into thinking that most teenagers are having sex. They aren't!) Others have sex because it is fun. They say, "If it feels good, why not?"

But do these reasons really make sense? Will having sex make you more popular or give you true friendships?

By having sex before you're married, you are not showing your maturity; you are actually showing that you are immature, because you are doing something that God forbids. God tells us the only way to be prepared for sex is to make the commitments that are made in a wedding ceremony. There is a lot to know and think about before you say yes to having sex.

Take a look at what God has to say about sex:

God wants you to be holy and pure and to keep clear of all sexual sin so that each of you will marry in holiness and honor.
1 THESSALONIANS 4:3-4, TLB

Being pure in our sexual behavior is a characteristic of genuine Christians. Nicole, there are other verses that you can look at to see that God has designed sex for marriage. But let me give you some more reasons to remain a virgin in addition to the most important one—because God says to.

Ten reasons to remain a virgin until you are married

1. To protect yourself from making the physical and sexual part of life too big a deal. This part of life can easily begin to control us and cause us great pain and grief.
2. To protect yourself from distrust in marriage. If you

give in to the sex pull now, you will live with the question in your mind, *Will I be able to control my sex life when I am married?* It's a painful and awkward spot to be in when you look at your husband on your wedding night and say, "Honey, I give you myself, but you aren't the first."

3. To protect yourself from guilt and anger. If you avoid having sex while you are unmarried, you will save yourself a truckload of guilt and a boxcar of anger.
4. To protect yourself from low self-esteem. Every teen I know who has had premarital sex has a lower view of themselves because they gave in to sexual temptation.
5. To protect yourself from the risk of pregnancy. Unless you are ready to be a mommy, stay away from sex.
6. To protect yourself from medical problems such as sexually transmitted diseases. We've talked about how destructive AIDS can be, plus there are other diseases that can be very painful and damaging.
7. To protect yourself from emotional problems like depression.
8. To protect yourself from a perverted or depraved mind (Romans 1). Playing around with sex can make you really obsessed with it.
9. To protect yourself from a cold conscience. If you are willing to ignore God's truth in this area of your life, you probably will become quite hard in other areas as well. This can lead to a real callousness towards God and his Word.
10. To protect yourself from sexual confusion and homosexuality. People who experiment with sex early often have bad experiences. This negative "first time" can cause such strong negative images that some teens are actually repelled in their minds about having sex with someone of the opposite sex.

There you have it, Nicole: ten reasons to stay a virgin until your wedding night. And all of these show that God's command makes a lot of sense. Remember, God never asks you to do anything that he won't be there to help you with.

I'm looking forward to that special day when you dress in white and get married. Make sure you give me plenty of warning—I need to save some cash!

Love,

Dad

(Future Father of the Bride)

What do you think?

Why do you think God designed rules to go along with his design for sex?

_____

_____

_____

_____

_____

Designer Sex—Doing It God's Way

THIRTEEN

True love waits. Love is patient.

—DAD

Dear Nicole,

I admire you for taking a stand with your friends about premarital sex. If they ask you, "Why is God down on premarital sex?" what would you say?

God isn't down on sex! He's excited about it! After all, he invented it! His concern is simply that we use sex as it was created to be used. When we follow the Creator's instructions, we get the maximum enjoyment and fulfillment out of sex. When we ignore God's instructions and plans, we wind up feeling empty inside, and we miss the real joy of sex.

I remember talking to Karen, a fourteen-year-old girl who was talked into having sex by her sixteen-year-old boyfriend. Karen told me, "It really wasn't even that much fun. I was scared, it hurt, and I felt so used, dirty, and guilty afterwards. So what's the big deal about sex? It really was no big thrill!"

Nicole, God intended sex to be fun—and, yes, thrilling! But he created us to best express love and enjoy sex within the security of marriage. Sex is more than "making love," it is an expression of love and self-control. When a husband and wife control themselves in such a way that they save sex for each other—and no one else—then it becomes a very special, unique gift that they give each other. This develops a wonderful bond that is different from any other relationship. When sex is outside of marriage, this special bond is impossible. Outside of marriage, sex can become more of a noose than a bond. Listen to what Tom (age fourteen) says about it:

"We started foolin' around a little, and before you knew it we were going all the way. It was kind of exciting at first, but it made us both feel guilty and trapped. It was almost like being hooked on a drug—every time we got together we started foolin' around. After a while it really wasn't that much fun, but we couldn't stop."

What does God think about this?

It is God's will that you should be holy: that you should avoid sexual immorality; that each of you should learn to control his own body in a way that is holy and honorable.
1 THESSALONIANS 4:3-4

Sounds pretty clear to me. God wants us to actively *avoid* sexual immorality. It's not enough just to keep from doing it; we should be active in avoiding situations that may lead to sexual sin. This includes all sorts of things, such as watching movies or reading books and magazines that cause you to think about sex. Sometimes we need to actually run away from situations that may tempt us sexually.

Flee the evil desires of youth, and pursue righteousness, faith, love and peace, along with those who call on the Lord out of a pure heart.
2 TIMOTHY 2:22

Nicole, controlling your body is *your* responsibility. No one else can do it for you. God holds you responsible for what you do with your sex life. To be involved sexually before marriage is against his will. But God never asks us to do anything that he doesn't give us the strength to do.

You also need to realize, Nicole, that boys are sexually aroused by sight, as well as by touch. This means that it is unfair for girls to dress immodestly. Fashion wants girls to dress alluringly, to attract boys' looks and sexual interest. But this is not the way of purity.

No temptation has seized you except what is common to man. And God is faithful; he will not let you be tempted beyond what you can bear. But when you are tempted, he will also provide a way out so that you can stand up under it.

1 CORINTHIANS 10:13

If sex before marriage is an option for you, then saying no is difficult—especially when you have friends who say, "Go for it, don't be weird!" But God tells us not to, and he has good reasons. He also helps us live with the pressure and provides a "way out so that you can stand up under it."

As you can tell, Nicole, 1 Corinthians 10:13 is one of my favorite verses. I guess it's because I use it all the time.

Struggling with sexual issues doesn't end in your teen years—it only begins there! But the lessons you learn as a young teen can help you the rest of your life.

A fellow learner,

Dad

What do you think?

If God promises "a way out" of sexual temptation, what could be some of those "escape routes"?

_____

_____

_____

_____

_____

Bridle that Tongue!

FOURTEEN

If you judge people, you have no time to love them.

—MOTHER TERESA

Dear Nicole,

"She's such a whiny, insecure person! She practically lies all over the guys when she's talking to them. 'Oh! I'm so tired,' she says, and lays her head on their shoulder. Disgusting!"

Janet threw herself over Mark's lap, mimicking Rachel. We were on a Car Rally with the high school group, and Janet was talking about Rachel's behavior.

"Doesn't she have a clue that she's being so obvious? I mean she acts so desperate! She's—"

"Wow, Janet, would you like her raggin' on you like you're doing to her?" asked Allison, riding shotgun.

"Yeah, it makes you wonder what she says about *you* behind your back, Allison," I said.

Allison shrugged in agreement.

"I'm not saying anything that isn't true!" Janet objected.

"Getting a little defensive there, Janet?" Mark asked sarcastically.

"I'm not the one with the problem. She's the one that's weird, or I wouldn't be talking about her!" exclaimed Janet.

Nicole, this conversation happened this week in our car. I was glad to see Allison stand up to Janet, her best friend, and question her gossiping. Her courage reminded me of you. It takes courage to admit that our words can get us into trouble. I've seen you do that.

When we start talking about others, it's easy to gossip.

Deep down we know it is wrong, but we can't seem to stop. The Bible describes the tongue as the most unmanageable part of the body.

The tongue is a small part of the body, but it makes great boasts . . . a world of evil among the parts of the body. It corrupts the whole person, sets the whole course of his life on fire.
JAMES 3:5-6

In other words, you are what you say.

Nicole, have you ever noticed that when you start ripping on someone, it makes you feel better about yourself? Why does gossiping make you feel better? Because you pick out something critical about someone and exaggerate it. For a little while you feel superior to that person, but it doesn't last.

Janet was picking on Rachel for her behavior with boys. Actually, I think she was jealous. When someone seems to have things you don't, you may put her down so you will feel better.

The challenge is to try to say something positive about a person—even if you have to work at it.

Do not let any unwholesome talk come out of your mouths, but only what is helpful for building others up according to their needs, that it may benefit those who listen.
EPHESIANS 4:29

Our words are to be *wholesome*. This means we should use words that "promote health." They are to build others up, add good things to their lives. Also, they are to benefit the listener.

Face it, all of us like to hear dirt about others, but afterwards we feel a little dirty ourselves. Picture it this way. Imagine you are four years old and you are carefully building with your blocks. (Remember those big blocks in preschool?) Another kid comes along and has a choice: to add to what you are building, or to pull out a block and knock the whole thing down.

That is the choice you make with how you use words: Build up or tear down.

Another tip that has helped me, Nicole, is when you start to talk about someone, picture that person right beside you. That will quickly put out the fire in your tongue!

Nicole, you've inherited the gift of talk from me. It can be useful at times, and it can be a real pain too. I hope these ideas help you; they've helped me put a bridle on my tongue. A little bit steers the whole horse!

Love,

Dad

What do you think?

Is it realistic to say something positive about a person instead of gossiping about them?

_____

_____

_____

_____

_____

Phil's Philosophy

Opportunity comes disguised as a problem.

—Dad

FIFTEEN

Dear Nicole,

Mom told me that some kids at school were teasing you for
what you believe. I'm sorry that happened. Why would they
do that?

You know that being a Christian doesn't mean your life will
be easy. God doesn't push the delete button on all your problems. Sometimes being a Christian *creates* problems.

Do you remember Phil in the high school group? Phil really
wanted to start standing up for God at school. One day his
teacher assigned a paper called "My Life Philosophy." Phil told
me it was due in two weeks and that the teacher would have
some of the students read their papers in front of the class. Phil
also told me that he intended to tell people about his faith in
Christ and how that is the basis for his philosophy of life.

I wasn't sure if Phil would do it. At other times he talked
about "sticking up for God and gettin' radical," but he didn't
come through. This time he did. Phil wrote a five-hundred-
word paper telling how God had changed his life. He
described how he used to like getting into trouble and basically
showing off. Since he met Jesus, he was now living for God
and not for himself.

Nicole, the teacher was so impressed with Phil's paper that
she asked him to read it in front of the class. Phil was very
nervous as he read it, because he knew that some people never
had a clue that he knew God. But as he read it, God gave him

strength and boldness. People stared at him as he told them, "God is Number One in my life."

At lunch that day some of Phil's friends called him "preacher," "padre," and "brother." They were putting him down for his statement about his faith. The next day, some of his friends avoided him, and he had to eat lunch alone. This went on for several days. If it weren't for his brother, Phil would have eaten lunch alone for weeks.

When we stand up for God it can cost us. Friends. Popularity. Teasing. Weird looks.

Phil would tell you that it was worth it. Because he stood up for God that first time, it became easier later. Before too long, Phil's friends came back to him and asked why his faith meant so much to him. They asked how he could have "peace inside" when they were so angry or troubled. Phil was able to talk to them about his relationship with Jesus.

Phil learned that many opportunities come disguised as problems. He decided to take a risk for God.

Sometimes we become more concerned with our comfort than our convictions. We'd rather be comfortable than right. But being a Christian means doing the right thing, even if it isn't easy.

Praise the Lord if you are punished for doing right!
1 PETER 2:19, TLB

I wish things were different for you, Nicole. I wish that when you were being picked on, you could clap your hands and a six-foot-six bodyguard would appear and protect you! But I guess you do have a Bodyguard, and he's with you *all* the time. That helps your anxious dad relax!

Anxiously yours,

Dad

What do you think?

If you were given the same assignment as Phil, what would you say is your life philosophy?

_____

_____

_____

_____

_____

Jimmy—The Party Animal

SIXTEEN

*Wounds from a friend are better
than kisses from an enemy!*

—PROVERBS 27:6,TLB

Dear Nicole,

The unmistakable aroma of marijuana drifted in from our
neighbor's yard. As I vacuumed our pool, the scent took me
back to high school. I thought of Jimmy—the party animal.

Jimmy was a popular freshman at my high school. He
excelled at football and was expected to make varsity his
sophomore year.

Jimmy always went to the football parties—the ones on Fri-
day night after the varsity game. There he learned to talk big,
walk big, and drink big.

It was kind of funny to see Jimmy acting big because he was
short and brawny; a definite "wide-body." At these parties,
Jimmy liked to show off for the varsity players and cheerlead-
ers. He wanted them to notice him. He wanted them to accept
him. To get their attention he'd drink too much beer and then
do hula dances without his shirt. He would dive off the roof
into the pool. He would pick fights with people.

He was running out of attention-getting things to do
towards the end of the year, so he started showing up at these
parties with several joints (marijuana cigarettes). He'd share
them with his friends, wear sunglasses even though it was
night, and laugh continuously. It seemed like Jimmy was having
a great time. We all laughed. We laughed at Jimmy his
sophomore year, his junior year, and then it hit us—Jimmy was
hooked on marijuana! No laughing matter. To get up in the

morning he needed "just one quick one." To handle the pressure of third period he'd light up out in the parking lot between classes. At lunch he'd relax with friends at the beach and smoke a few joints. After school he usually worked out, went home, did thirty minutes of homework, and then took off somewhere to smoke some more.

Nicole, my friend had become an addict right in front of my eyes. What should I have done? I didn't know. But here are some things I know now, in case you face something like this with one of your friends:

1. Decide which is more important: having your friend like you, or doing what is best for her. If you want her to like you and you really don't care about her or her health, then let it go—do nothing.
2. If you care about your friend, then let her know it. Say, "I like you—you are a good friend."
3. At another time say it again, but this time say, "I care about you and want you to know I'm worried about you." Express your concern about her smoking marijuana (or drinking alcohol, or whatever it is).
4. Ask her why she does it. Also ask if you can still be friends with her if you don't use marijuana (or whatever).
5. If you are close friends, ask her to stop—or at least consider stopping—as a favor to you. Pray for your friend to lose her desire for the thing she's addicted to.
6. If your friend ignores you or is rude to you, talk to Mom or me or another adult who can give you some advice. (Try the youth worker at church.)
7. Be willing to do a little private-eye work to find out how often your friend uses marijuana, where, with whom, and where she gets it.

8. After you have done your detective work, write it down, go to your friend, and say, "I've told you I care about you and I'm still worried about you using marijuana. I know that you are using it (when) with (whom), and you buy from (dealer). I really want you to consider what you're doing to yourself. Remember, I care about you." Don't threaten to turn her into the police, school, or parents—at least not yet.
9. Pray for your friend to feel guilty and worried about her drug abuse. Also pray for an opportunity to talk with her when she's serious and sober.
10. Consider teen drug-recovery programs you can help your friend get to that don't require money or parents' permission.
11. If your friend doesn't try to stop and won't work with you on it, then you might try love—tough love. Two strategies to try: (1) Let her know you'll need to put some space between you and her because of her substance abuse. (2) Get her some help for her problem. Talk to your youth worker, counselor, or teacher.
12. Be willing to trust God to give you a new friend, one who is healthy and drug-free.

Nicole, sometimes the most helpful and loving thing we can do for a friend is to get them in trouble. Actually, they *are* in trouble and you are getting them in touch with someone who can help.

Sometimes I've found it helpful to say, "I've tried all kinds of things to help you [tell them the steps you took], but you just don't seem to care. I'm angry and disappointed, but I'll give you one more try. If you're willing to get help, I'll stay with you. But if you aren't, I'm going to need to get some help by telling someone." This is playing hardball, but for some, it is the only way. If you love a person, you'll do what's best for them, even though they may hate you for it.

Nicole, we will be glad to help you deal with this problem when it comes up. But I wanted to give you these twelve steps in case you weren't comfortable coming to us about it. At least you'll have my thoughts from this letter. I've seen a lot of teenagers mess up their lives with drugs. I've also seen God use loving friends like you to reach out and get help for friends with a substance-abuse problem.

Chances are you'll have a friend like Jimmy. I hope you'll know what to do—I didn't.

Love,

Dad

What do you think?

Do you know people like Jimmy, the Party Animal? Do you know someone who could become like Jimmy?

_____

_____

_____

_____

_____

Black and White in a Gray World

In matters of style, swim with the current;
in matters of principle, stand like a rock.

—THOMAS JEFFERSON

Dear Nicole,

At times, life is confusing. It's hard to know right from wrong.
Maybe you find yourself asking, "Isn't there a happy medium?"

Imagine it is the lunch hour and you are surrounded by kids
talking. Swearwords come out as naturally as any other word.
You try to shut your ears to them but you can't.

*One of these days I'm going to slip and swear at home and then I'll
be in for it!* you think to yourself. You're torn between what we
(your mom and dad) expect and what you hear other kids saying. One part of you says it's wrong to swear, but the other
part of you wants to fit in with everybody else. You wish there
was a "happy medium," a middle of the road you could walk.
Well, there is a "medium," but it is not happy. It leaves you
straddling the fence when it comes to the question Should I or
shouldn't I? The fence is an uncomfortable place to be because
you spend much of your time and energy trying to keep from
falling off.

For instance, the first time you swear, or cheat on a test, or
do something else you know is wrong, something twinges
inside you and you begin to lose your balance on the fence.
This is because God has placed within each of us a conscience,
the ability to distinguish between right and wrong. Romans
2:12-15 states, "Down in their hearts they know right from
wrong. God's laws are written within them; their own conscience accuses them" (TLB).

When the first swearword slips out, a warning bell goes off inside you. If you tune in to the warning, you will feel uncomfortable. This feeling is a twinge of guilt triggered by your conscience. But if you ignore the warning, it will grow fainter each time you swear and will finally be silent.

Nicole, this is what happens when you make excuses for yourself: "Everyone does it"; "It's so hard not to swear when you hear it all day." So you slip a little further and struggle to regain your balance on the fence.

This balancing act is difficult because nothing in your world is considered black or white; there are only shades of gray. A popular view is that no one else can tell you what is right or wrong; there are no set rules, you decide for yourself. Yet when there are no rules the result is confusion.

Imagine what would happen if the city removed all the traffic signals, stop signs, speed limit signs, and white lines from the streets on the way to your school. Cars and school buses would jockey for position. First they would jerk forward, then slam on their brakes. Horns would honk, tires would squeal, there would be confusion everywhere! How would you feel trying to get to school? No matter whether you were on the bus, walking, or riding your bicycle, you would be in real danger.

Nicole, this is a picture of a world without standards. That is why God was so wise to make things black and white, to give us standards to use in making choices.

The Bible doesn't come right out and say, "Thou shalt not go to the junior high dance" or "Buy the purple sundress." The Bible doesn't address every specific issue or decision, but it does give us principles that are general guidelines for making more specific decisions. For instance, the Bible doesn't say anything about rap music, but some rap is bad because the lyrics are violent, evil, and nasty. Scripture tells us to avoid all that is filthy and evil (James 1:21), so we need to avoid music that is not pure and moral.

Nicole, it is my prayer that God will help you make decisions on your own, based on biblical principles. If you have this skill, you can go anywhere and be prepared to make tough decisions.

Decidedly yours,
Dad

What do you think?

How does our conscience help us make decisions?

_____

_____

_____

_____

_____

The **B.E.S.T.** Music

A smile increases the property value of your face.
A song increases the mileage of your heart.

—DAD

Dear Nicole,

I'm glad you like music. I do too. It's fun to see you liking the
same kind of music I do, like DC Talk and Heather and Kir-
sten. But what about some of those groups you listen to on
your favorite radio station? Should a Christian listen to secular
rock?

Rock music is a hot issue in some circles. Some people are
convinced that all rock music is "a tool of the devil." Other
people use rock music to reach people and preach the gospel.
So why all the fuss? Why are so many people fighting over rock
music?

I believe that popular music can be helpful or it can be
destructive. The key is to evaluate the music you are listening
to.

Most teens like rock music. Their friends are totally into
rock. Not to like rock, for some people, is to commit social
suicide. But let's take a closer look. Forget about how popular it is and ask yourself, *What is it about this kind of music
that I like?* Is it the lyrics, the group's musical ability, their
cool looks, or what? Sometimes we listen to popular music
just because everyone else does.

I remember hearing a song on the radio while I was driving
a bus full of junior high students. I thought it was terrible. The
song was boring, the guy sang off-key, and the rhythm was
really weak. I thought it stunk! But the kids loved it. They said,

"That's such a hot hit!" Do you think everyone on that bus really did like the song, or do you think peer pressure has something to do with which songs are in?

The problem begins when a popular song talks about things that go against what the Bible says or what a Christian believes. I'm not saying, "Listen only to church organ and bell music." But we should think about the songs we listen to and the music we buy.

To help you evaluate what kind of music might be best for you as a Christian young person, consider the following:

The B.E.S.T. method of evaluating music

Build: Does this music build me up and make me a better person and a stronger Christian? The things that build up are those that help make me a servant and lead to unity. Ask yourself these questions: Does my music make me want to serve others or myself? Does my music lead to unity and peace (or is it bringing hassle with people and unrest in my mind)? Music is either building us up or tearing us down. Choose music that helps build you up.

Encourage: Does this music encourage me and others, or does it lead to discouragement and frustration? I believe it is wrong for Christians to do anything that discourages others from knowing God or being excited about all the good things God has done for us.

> *Let us therefore make every effort to do what*
> *leads to peace and to mutual edification.*
> ROMANS 14:19

Nicole, think about the music that you listen to. After listening for thirty minutes, do you feel more encouraged? If not, then maybe you shouldn't listen to it.

It's hard for Christian teens to be really encouraged by

music that goes against God. That's why some rock music leads to a kind of war inside the Christian teen. There's no peace inside because the message of the song doesn't fit with God, who lives inside you.

Stumble: Does this music cause me or others to stumble or trip when it comes to understanding God or a relationship with him?

Make up your mind not to put any stumbling block or obstacle in your brother's way. It is better not to eat meat or drink wine or to do anything else that will cause your brother to fall.
ROMANS 14:13, 21

Would others have questions about your faith if they heard you listening to this music? In other words, would they say, "What is a Christian doing listening to music like that?" If something we do causes someone to criticize Christians, or if it confuses them about what a Christian is, then we should ask ourselves if we really have the freedom to be involved in that activity.

Nicole, even though we have the "right" to do a lot of things as Christians, at times we need to give up that right so others won't be offended or confused. Sometimes music can really cause people to question our friendship with God. If others look at our music and they do not see something different from teens who do not know God, then something is wrong. We don't have to be weird, but they should be able to see God in our lives and in our music.

Tell: Does my music help tell about my relationship with God and all the great things he has done for me and the world? Does it make God look good, or does it call attention to me? Sometimes we listen to music because we want others to notice us. "Hey, look at that dude with the boom box and the hot tunes!"

We all want to be noticed, and music is one way of getting others to look at us. As Christians, it is our job to make God look good. The Bible calls this "glorifying God." It means to point the spotlight on God and call attention to who he is and what he has done for us. If all we ever listen to is music that makes us look cool or makes us fit in with our friends, we may never point others to God.

So whether you eat or drink or whatever
you do, do it all for the glory of God.
1 CORINTHIANS 10:31

Nicole, one of the *best* ways to do this is to listen to contemporary Christian music. There are all kinds of styles; hip-hop, rap, heavy metal, speed, thrash, pop, dance, folk, alternative, and country. If they play it on the radio, you can bet there is a Christian band that sounds similar. A lot of these groups make music that passes the B.E.S.T. test. Check it out. Compare your music and some contemporary Christian music with these four ideas.

BEST tunes 4 you,
Dad

What do you think?

Do you think music has very much influence on you? Why?

_____

_____

_____

_____

_____

Staying Close to God

NINETEEN

As the deer pants for streams of water, so my soul pants
for you, O God. My soul thirsts for God, for the living God.
When can I go and meet with God?

—PSALM 42:1-2

Dear Nicole,

It was fun to help you with your Bible study on wisdom
tonight. I know you have a heart for God's Word—you did the
whole week's assignment the first night of Bible school! But
what can you do if you get bored with spiritual things?

If you are like a lot of young people, you really do want to
have a better relationship with God, but sometimes you find it
hard to get motivated to do anything about it. Getting excited
about studying the Bible and praying is sometimes as difficult
as getting excited about doing your math homework. It just
isn't exciting!

Why is it important to have a stronger spiritual life? Most of
us would respond to that question by saying that God is important to us and is worth the effort. Having a close friendship
with God requires the same things that it does to have a close
friendship with another person. You need to spend time with
each other, you have to talk to each other, and you need to
have common interests or things you can do with each other.

Start looking at spending time with God as an appointment
that you both look forward to. (He certainly looks forward to
it!) Nicole, when I have an appointment with a friend, I don't
allow other things to crowd in on our time together.

When we spend time alone with God, we need to deal with
the problems and joys we are facing in life. If we don't, our

appointments with God become boring religious duties. Daughter, here are some tips for your appointment with God:

1. Decide on a time when you are alert and free from distractions. Try to have your appointment three or four times a week (more would be even better).
2. Begin your appointment with prayer. Say, "Dear God, I ask you to help me understand you and your Word. Help me to learn something and to change something in my life. Amen." When we are ready to change things, we are ready to grow.
3. Spend time with cats. That's right, c-a-t-s! This is an acrostic that has helped me in my quiet times. It helps me balance things and not treat God like Santa Claus—you know, "I want this, and I want that. . . ."

   Confession means saying the same thing that God does about sin—he hates it! It means telling God about sin in your life and agreeing to make some changes about it.

   Adoration means expressing our appreciation for the wonder and awesomeness of who God *is*. It is saying, "God, I value how you have forgiven me, how patient you have been with me, and how powerful you really are. . . ."

   Thanksgiving means telling God "thanks" for the many things he has done for me and for others. This is different from adoration, which focuses on who God *is*. Thanksgiving focuses on what God *does*.

   Supplication comes from the word *supply*. It means asking God to supply different needs we might have or asking God to meet the needs of others.

But spending time reading the Bible and praying is not all there is to the Christian life; it is just *part* of the Christian's life.

God is with us wherever we are. We spend the whole day with him. (He spends the whole day with us!) We don't need to spend five minutes in "devotions" and then forget about God the rest of the day.

Take God with you when you pick out your clothes for the day. Ask him to help you choose clothes that will make you and him look good. Then take God with you to school. Begin the day by asking him to help you stay alert and listen to what is being said. When you are talking to your friends, ask God to help them with their problems, and thank him that you have friends.

Nicole, these are a few things that I have found to work, but the most important thing in staying close to God is honestly telling him how you feel. If you are angry, tell him. If you are worried, let him know. You won't surprise him! When we are honest about our emotions it makes us close to someone. Take the risk of faith and be honest about your feelings with God. He totally understands, even more than I do.

With you in the journey,

Dad

What do you think?

Think back on a time when you felt close to God. What made you feel that way?

_____

_____

_____

_____

_____

Party On, Dude!

TWENTY

Wine is a mocker and beer a brawler;
whoever is led astray by them is not wise.

—PROVERBS 20:1

Dear Nicole,

During the houseboat trip, one of the campers told me that at home she had been going to parties where kids were drinking alcohol. As a Christian, she wanted to know, "Is it OK to drink if I don't get drunk?"

"The pressure to drink is growing," I agreed. "At many parties for junior highers, beer is available. Many will drink it, others won't. Some pretend to get drunk, some will get drunk. In our city we've had a lot of deaths due to teenage drinking."

"Yeah, so have we. One guy got shot, and a car full of kids got in a crash and killed all four."

Nicole, you may have the urge to drink. If you do, ask yourself, *Why do I want to drink?* Is it to look cool? Is it because other friends are? Or is it because you're thirsty and like the taste of beer? My guess is that if you have the urge to drink someday, it will be to look cool and do what your friends are doing.

The Bible is our guidebook to life, but it doesn't have specific instructions that say "junior highers shalt not drink beer!" Instead, it gives us some principles—some guidelines to live by. Let's take a look at some of them.

We are to obey our parents (you knew I'd work this in!).

Children, obey your parents in the Lord, for this is right. "Honor

your father and mother"—which is the first commandment with a promise—"that it may go well with you and that you may enjoy long life on the earth. "
EPHESIANS 6:1-3

"Obey your parents in the Lord" means to obey your parents as you would obey God, because he put them in that position. When we follow our parents' wishes we really are following God. If our parents don't want us drinking alcohol then we shouldn't. Most parents realize the dangers of alcohol and restrict their teen from drinking it. This is wise, because teenagers often will do silly things because of peer pressure. Mixing alcohol with peer pressure can be a deadly combination. That's why obeying our parents can make our lives more enjoyable and longer.

We are to obey the government.

Everyone must submit himself to the governing authorities, for there is no authority except that which God has established. The authorities that exist have been established by God. Consequently, he who rebels against the authority is rebelling against what God has instituted, and those who do so will bring judgment on themselves.
ROMANS 13:1-2

Another principle from the Bible is to obey the authorities God places over us. To rebel against the police or the laws of the school or state is to fight against God. In our country (in most states), it is illegal for teenagers to buy and consume alcohol. For a young person to drink is to be in violation of city or state laws. In some areas, it's legal for teens to drink in their own home under a parent's supervision—but most kids drink at parties at someone else's home without any parents around. The second principle is important to follow because these laws have been written to protect people from hurting themselves and others.

We are to do things that help others—not hurt them.

It is better not to eat meat or drink wine or to do anything else that will cause your brother to fall.
ROMANS 14:21

If you want to throw out the first two principles because they sound stupid to you, then you'll have to figure out what to do with Romans 14. The whole chapter talks about having the freedom to do things (like eating certain foods and drinking alcohol) but choosing not to do them because it causes other Christians to fall. Paul is talking about the fact that some early Christians felt free to eat discount meat that had been offered to pagan idols. It was cheaper and they could then give more money to the church. But other Christians thought it was terrible that they were eating "contaminated" food. The truth was that nothing was wrong with the food or with eating it. They had the freedom to eat it, but because it caused problems for others they decided not to.

Nicole, this is a tricky principle to apply to our lives, but the main idea is to think of others before we just go ahead and do what we like. If you were to sip on a beer at a party, even though you don't get drunk, the word may get out that you were drinking at a party where people got drunk. If you claim to be a Christian, this will look bad because Christians aren't supposed to get drunk (Ephesians 5:18).

Avoid every kind of evil.
1 THESSALONIANS 5:22)

We are encouraged to avoid even the appearance of evil.

Sometimes we have to steer clear of situations that make others think we're involved in things that are wrong. It's not the easy option—but it is the loving one. Sometimes being a Christian means giving up our freedom so people don't get the wrong idea.

That's what I told her, Nicole. She smiled and said it helped, but I'll probably never see her again. I wonder how she's doing? I wish I could talk with her to find out.

I *can* talk with you, though! We've talked before about drinking and drugs. Let's keep the conversation going. I want to hear your opinions on the topic, too.

Love,

Dad

What do you think?

What is your opinion on teenage drinking? What would you tell your friends if they asked you?

_____

_____

_____

_____

_____

Power of the Sprayed Word

Graffiti: Wit and run literature.

—BOB PHILLIPS

Dear Nicole,

Remember when we were driving on the Hollywood Freeway
and saw all the graffiti? Brooke asked, "What's wrong with graffiti?" I gave her a quick response, but here is a little more on
the topic. Which one of these statements is closest to your
opinion on graffiti?

- Graffiti is a creative expression of teenagers' emotions.
- Graffiti is malicious vandalism done by hoodlums.
- Graffiti is modern art, like Picasso.
- Graffiti is vengeance on a wall.

Nicole, there are many different views on graffiti. Some
experts say it's good for teenagers to express themselves;
others want to throw you in jail for putting a little paint on an
ugly, boring fence.

Under a bridge near our house reads some graffiti: "Don't
destroy the work of Sandman. This is not graffiti, it is art.
Please leave it alone. Sandman was killed in an accident August
8. Please respect his work." Above this warning are some artis-
tic graphics. Every day students walk on the path under the
bridge to go to school. I wonder what they think?

I'm all for creative art done on walls and bridges with the
permission of the owners. In fact, many ugly, bland concrete

surfaces have been dressed up by the talents of these street Rembrandts in high-tops.

But how would you feel, Nicole, if you were the owner of a building I recently noticed? The owner had just painted over hundreds of profane and obscene words on this huge wall. It probably cost him thousands of dollars. Local citizens were delighted because now we could drive by without feeling our minds were being attacked. But three days later, the graffiti began to reappear—bigger and more obscene than ever. Why should we be forced to view that stuff?

Graffiti (or "tagging") bothers me because most of it feels like an invasion of privacy. It forces me to think about foul words, suicide, gang wars, sex outside marriage, and problems of people I don't even know. It creates tension inside those who read it because it often offends or disturbs, and we don't know how to reach out to those who write it.

My guess is that a lot of youths do it out of anger. Many others may be bored and looking for something fun and daring to do. Graffiti is cheap thrills at the expense of others.

A lot of graffiti is advertising for gangs who are "tagging" their turf. When gang members spray-paint their tag on a wall, it gives them a sense of pride. Taggers join tagging crews to give them a sense of identity and being on a team. In a way, it's a family. Taggers often come from families that don't work too well. In their tagging crew they discover they can be noticed and even important.

What do you think about graffiti? Right? Wrong? Depends? Nicole, think about the typical graffiti message and compare it with the following Scripture. Maybe that will help shape your opinion.

Wisdom will save you from the ways of wicked men, from men whose words are perverse, who leave the straight paths to walk in dark

ways, who delight in doing wrong and rejoice in the perverseness of evil, whose paths are crooked and are devious in their ways.
PROVERBS 2:12-15

Even though I've said all of this, give me a clean wall and a can of spray paint and I must admit I'd be tempted to write "I LOVE NICOLE" in four-foot letters!

Proudly yours,
Dad

What do you think?

How does graffiti make you feel? How does it make observers feel? How does it make the owner of the wall feel?

_____

_____

_____

_____

_____

Dear Nicole,

I know that at school kids swear and use bad language. We've talked about this. You may ask yourself, *How can I keep from swearing?* Here are my thoughts.

Most of us know the rule:

> *You shall not misuse the name of the Lord your God, for the Lord will not hold anyone guiltless who misuses his name.*
> EXODUS 20:7

Why is it that people use *Jesus Christ* or *God* as swearwords? Because they are powerful words. People who usually feel a little weak try to make themselves look stronger by using strong language. Someone once said, "Swearing is an attempt by a feeble mind to come across as an authority" (*feeble* means weak). In some ways it does make sense to use God's name instead of a person's. Can you imagine using the name *Harry* as a swearword? It wouldn't carry much weight! People must know that God's name is powerful, or they wouldn't use it when they swear.

Let's say your name is Julie. How would you like it if people, when they got mad, would spit out, *"Julieee!"* At first you might keep saying, "Yes, what do you want?" But after a while it would get old, and it would make you mad. You'd probably respond with, "Don't use my name unless you want me!" The same is true with God and Jesus. We are not supposed to misuse their names.

But I tell you, Do not swear at all: either by heaven, for it is God's throne; or by the earth, for it is his footstool. . . . Simply let your "Yes" be "Yes," and your "No," "No."
MATTHEW 5:34-37

Nicole, if you catch yourself using God's name in swearing, you might want to ask yourself some questions:

1. Where did I first learn to do this?
2. Am I copying someone I want to be like or trying to impress them?
3. Am I trying to sound cool or tough by swearing?
4. Since I am a Christian and have a relationship with God, how does misusing his name affect that relationship?

What about those other "swearwords"? You know, the ones that are called "four-letter words" and are profane or obscene (dirty). Is it right for a Christian kid to let a few of these rip from time to time?

Think about your favorite bad word—the one that sometimes sneaks out of your lips. Got it in mind? I've got one in mind that I slip up on. Nicole, let's see how our favorite bad words stack up against the following Scripture:

Do not let any unwholesome talk come out of your mouths, but only what is helpful for building others up according to their needs, that it may benefit those who listen.
EPHESIANS 4:29

Is it wholesome (pure)? Does it help to build others up and encourage them? Do people benefit by hearing you use that word? If not, then it's a good word to weed from your vocabulary. Swearwords are like dandelions—if you let a few in, they'll take over. (Kind of like our backyard!) Here are some tips on weeding out the swearwords:

1. Try to count how many times you use a swearword in one morning or afternoon.
2. Make a list of the words you want to stop using.
3. Ask God to help you erase these words from your mind and your lips.
4. Every day meditate (concentrate) on a verse from the Bible. (I'd suggest Philippians 4:8.)
5. When you catch yourself swearing, stop—tell God you are sorry, thank him for forgiving you, and then ask him to help you stop.
6. Cross out a swearword on your list when you can get through a week without saying it.
7. Ask a friend to wink at you or tug on her left earlobe when she catches you swearing. (This beats her saying out loud, "I thought you were going to stop swearing!")
8. Stop allowing the input of swearwords as much as you can. Watch your choice of movies, music, jokes, and even friends.

Nicole, we'll help you too. If we hear you using bad language, we'll probably point it out. And to be totally fair, if I blow it with bad language, I'd like you to let me know (privately is best). Sometimes we don't even realize we're doing it. It can become a bad habit that we aren't aware of.

Here's to good words!

Love,

Dad

What do you think?

What do you think about the eight tips for weeding out swear-words? Are they realistic? Helpful? Impossible?

_____

_____

_____

_____

_____

Gorgeous Toes

TWENTY-THREE

Share with your friends the most important thing in your life.
You will open the window to your heart.

—DAD

Dear Nicole,

I know that some of your friends are Christians, but I also
know some aren't. Do you ever ask yourself, *How do I tell my
friends about Jesus?*

Make sure your feet are beautiful. That's right—if you want
to tell your friends about Jesus, you'll need beautiful tootsies!

> *As it is written, "How beautiful are the feet of*
> *those who bring good news!"*
> ROMANS 10:15

Doesn't that sound weird? But think about it. Imagine you
are a farmer whose crops are dying, and you're almost starving
because of drought. A barefoot stranger hikes twenty miles to
your farm and says, "There's a big rainstorm coming this afternoon!" You notice the callouses and blisters on the stranger's
feet. The toes are fat and flat from walking without shoes. You
think to yourself, *How worn and ugly! Why doesn't he—*

Crash! Thunder breaks the silence; lightning bolts divide the
sky. It begins to pour. The barefoot stranger cracks a smile and
nods. You begin to cry, but glancing down at his feet, through
your tears, you notice something—his feet are beautiful!

What happened in this story? The ugly, worn feet of the
stranger became beautiful because they were used to spread
good news.

Nicole, I think it's interesting that God did not say, "How beautiful are the *mouths* of those who bring good news." He was emphasizing feet for a reason. Feet take us places. They can be used for dancing or kicking. Feet can get us into trouble, or they can get us out of trouble. Where a person allows his feet to take him tells what is important to him.

If our goal is simply to *tell* our friends about the Good News, they'll probably ignore us. If we remember that our "feet"—our behavior and attitudes—also communicate Jesus, our friends will be more apt to listen.

If you confess with your mouth, "Jesus is Lord," and believe in your heart that God raised him from the dead, you will be saved.
ROMANS 10:9

Nicole, as you can see from this verse, it is not enough to talk about Jesus. We need to make him our Lord and believe that he is alive and lives within us.

Here are some questions to think about as you consider a makeover for beautiful feet:

1. If Jesus is your Lord, he is Number One in your life. Nothing else, no one else, comes first. How can you show that Jesus is your Lord?
2. Why is it important to believe that Jesus was raised from the dead? (To prove that he is stronger than sin or death.)
3. How well do you know the Good News? Your friends will be more excited to respond to good news than bad news. What is the Good News of Jesus? (That Jesus loves everyone, and when he died on the cross he opened the door for us to have a relationship with God.)
4. Take a look at John 3:16 and Romans 5:8 for more good news about Jesus.

5. If you want to tell your friends about Jesus, all you have to do is tell them what happened to you. Here are three things to say:

- Briefly describe your life *before* you met Jesus (for instance, you might mention feeling guilty or not having peace).
- Tell them *how* you met Jesus (where you were, what you said, what you prayed).
- Tell them what *changes* Jesus has made in your life (made you more forgiving, gave you peace, etc.).

You might want to throw in a few verses like Romans 3:23, 1 John 1:9, or Romans 6:23. But the important thing to do is tell them *your* good-news story and leave the rest to God!

Nicole, you have such a warm and friendly personality. God will use you to introduce himself to your friends.

Joyfully,
Dad

What do you think?

What do you think about the statement "Where a person allows his feet to take him tells what is important to him"?

_____

_____

_____

_____

_____

Top Ten Reasons Not to Grow Up

TWENTY-FOUR

*Three stonecutters were asked what they were doing.
The first said, "I'm cutting this stone into blocks." The second
one said, "I'm working to feed my family." The third
stonecutter enthusiastically exclaimed,
"I'm building a magnificent cathedral to the glory of God!"*

—DAD

Dear Nicole,

Do you ever feel like you are in-between? Not a kid, and not
an adult? Somedays you probably don't feel like growing up.

"I don't want to grow up 'cuz I'm a Toys 'R' Us kid" has
become a popular song—and feeling—these days. Why should
we want to grow up in a world full of problems? Some of them
are very serious. There are some good reasons to grow up and
become responsible. But here are ten reasons *not* to grow up:

Top ten reasons not to grow up

10. I like being dependent and provided for.
9. I like not having to make decisions.
8. I don't want the worry of making a fool of myself.
7. I've seen "responsible" people really mess up their
   lives.
6. Being a kid allows me to get by with more.
5. Being an irresponsible kid means I can hang around
   younger kids and push them around.
4. Why grow up so soon? I like being a kid.

3. I don't know what I want to be when I grow up, so I won't.
2. Growing up means not having any fun (adults have boring toys).
1. A lot of grown-ups act like kids, so what's the difference?

Which one is your favorite? These reasons not to grow up are kind of fun to think about, but sooner or later we have to face the music. There is no sense in acting like you're twelve when you are twenty.

At all ages, we want to feel like there is a place for us. We all want to feel like we have something to contribute. At the National Youth Workers Convention in 1992, I heard Tony Campolo say, "Young people are searching for meaning. They want to make a difference in their world. They want to do something that will count. They need a sense of mission—of destiny and purpose. Too many young people have no reason for their existence."

Nicole, do you feel you have a "sense of mission" in your life? A mission is something that demands our focus. To find out what your mission is, you must look at your heart.

Above all else, guard your heart, for it is the wellspring of life.
PROVERBS 4:23

The things that are close to your heart affect all parts of your life. That's why it is important to guard your affections and the things you live for (your wishes, dreams, etc.). The heart will show itself in good or bad behavior.

The good man brings good things out of the good stored up in his heart, and the evil man brings evil things out of the evil stored up in his heart. For out of the overflow of his heart his mouth speaks.
LUKE 6:45

Our heart will show what is really important to us (our *values*). Our values will affect our choices and our behavior. Nicole, take a minute to think through the following values. Which are the most important to you?

- popularity
- independence
- good grades
- friendship
- physical appearance
- leadership
- wealth
- happiness

Values are important, but they don't make much sense unless we know what our purpose is. Here's a formula that might help:

PURPOSE + VALUES = SIGNIFICANCE

Nicole, I believe a Christian's purpose is to glorify Christ with his life. *Glorify* means "to make God look good." We want to call people's attention to the goodness of God. Our purpose will shape our values. Having a feeling of significance means feeling like you are doing something important and needed with your life.

Remember when we went to Mexico on that mission? You loved it because you felt significant. You had a purpose, knew your values, and had a meaningful time. Plus, you made a friend—Leticia; remember her?

This is what I'm talking about. Part of growing up is determining what difference each of us can make as individuals.

I'm excited about you discovering what your mission in life is. You have so much to offer: inviting your friends to youth group, giving piggyback rides to the kids in Mexico, teaching kindergartners every Sunday at church. Nicole, you are a loving, caring, fun, young woman with a purpose.

Let's make a difference!

Dad

What do you think?

Read that first quote about the three stonecutters. How did their purpose shape their perspective?

_____

_____

_____

_____

_____

Where Will I Be Safe?

Violence is the sign of temporary weakness.

—JEAN JAURES

Dear Nicole,

When we watched the L.A. riots on TV, I was afraid and asked myself, *Is there any place in the world where I can be safe?* It seemed like a war had broken out only thirty-seven miles down the freeway. It was a frightening experience. Remember those days?

Today the world is an unsafe place to be. You may think to yourself, *I'd like to get out of crazy southern California and go to another country,* but many countries have terrorist activity in them—with terrorists targeting Americans! The number of airplane accidents has increased dramatically in the last few years, and even if you land safely, you could be a victim of a drive-by shooting on your way home.

Nicole, I'll never forget a time I was really afraid. I had taken a group of high school guys backpacking in the High Sierra. At Beck Lakes, we discovered twenty-foot waterfalls coming down from the lake.

"Did you know you can go behind these, and it's really cool?" I asked.

"Go ahead, Tim," they said. "It looks too big. You'll get crunched."

Five teens watched their youth pastor/guide dive in and swim under the chilly, crashing water. The waterfall was larger than I thought. The water was falling thirty feet, not twenty feet like I guessed. It was also thicker and wider than I had anticipated. I had a difficult time swimming through the pounding surge, but after several attempts I made it through.

Behind the falls I discovered a beautiful emerald cavern. I shouted back, "It's great in here, come on in!" But they couldn't hear me. I could see them, but they couldn't see me. I swam over to the mossy wall to find a ledge to rest on. The chill from the runoff of melting snow made me breathe fast and tire quickly.

To my horror, I found no ledge. With mounting anxiety, I swam frantically around the crashing chamber to find only mossy, vertical walls. I had been treading water for five or ten minutes, and I was fatiguing quickly.

I need to find a shallow spot, I decided.

I dove under the water in search of a rock, a branch, or a foothold to stand on. I dove again. Again. Again. The entire cavern was fifteen feet deep. No place to rest.

I'll have to swim out before I drown.

I pushed off the slimy wall and swam under water at about six feet down. The turbulence from the falls thrust me back into the cavern. I tried again at eight feet. Then at ten. Twelve. Fifteen.

I couldn't get out of this slimy, freezing pit! Again I tried pulling myself along the bottom at fifteen feet down, but the backwash from the falls kept pushing me back. It felt like a ton of pressure. I couldn't fight it.

Then I remembered God. In my terror I had forgotten him.

"God, help me survive. Rescue me from this water!"

I heard God whisper to me, "Give it up. I'll take care of you."

I knew what I needed to do. I took a deep breath and swam with all my strength towards the deafening falls. As the current hit me, I gave into it and let it pull me down. It slammed me to the bottom, and I let out all the air in my lungs.

I prayed, *I'm giving it up to you, God. I'm in your hands.*

The turbulent current tossed me around like I was inside a dryer at the laundromat. After a few minutes of being pommeled by the pounding force of the water, I passed out.

I drifted into some underwater current, which took me downstream and to the surface. My backpacking buddies pulled me from the water and laid me on a rock. They thought I was dead.

The waterfall was scary. But what was really scary was Steve attempting mouth-to-mouth resuscitation. I came to just as his lips were inches away!

In spite of my foolishness, I learned a great lesson.

When you pass through the waters, I will be with you; and when you pass through the rivers, they will not sweep over you. When you walk through the fire, you will not be burned.
ISAIAH 43:2

I learned that God is with us when we are in deep waters (or when we are in deep yogurt!).

I learned that security is not in a place, it's in a person. Wherever we go in life there will be waters, rivers, and fires. But we don't walk alone. God is with us. He is our source of protection. He is our refuge and strength.

Nicole, you are sure to encounter challenges that will make you feel like you are drowning in deep waters. I hope this true story helps you remember that the safest place to be is in the hands of Jesus!

We can be afraid in the High Sierra or in the streets of Los Angeles. When I saw the Los Angeles police being attacked, I began to wonder if their shields and helmets would protect them. It seemed like they were so vulnerable and that the world had gone crazy. Then God helped me remember that police can't always keep us safe, but our confidence must be in God, and in him alone.

God is our refuge and strength, an ever-present help in trouble.
Therefore we will not fear, though the earth give way and the
mountains fall into the heart of the sea. . . . The Lord Almighty is
with us.
PSALM 46:1-2, 7

"Though the earth give way and the mountains fall into the heart of the sea." This is a verse for Californians! This year we had the killer earthquake. The earth gave way. It was really frightening. We talked about our fears. The comfort we can have is that God is with us. He will not abandon us.

In his grip,
Dad

What do you think?

How does God (who is spirit) help us with things that are scary and physical (like earthquakes, fires, and water)?

_____

_____

_____

_____

_____

Rescue Me from My Teacher!

TWENTY-SIX

*It ain't what a man don't know that
makes him a fool, but what he does know that ain't so.*

—JOSH BILLINGS

Dear Nicole,

Tonight as I said good night, you exclaimed, "Only ten more days until we find out who our teachers are. I sure hope I don't get Mr. Mickowski; he's terrible!"

I know you are worried about what teachers you get. What should you do if you get a teacher you hate?

Imagine getting Mr. Mickowski. You'll drag yourself to class each day. If you could, you would hide out in the restroom. You'll sigh in defeat as you get back each assignment, *I cannot please him, no matter how hard I try.* Naturally, he calls on you right away. You stumble through an answer, then melt into your chair. He continues to yell and talk about confusing information.

Nicole, how do you make it through nine months of school with a teacher you hate? What do you do when you clash head-on with someone who makes you sick? (I've heard you complain about Mr. Mickowski!) Here are three things that might help:

- First, recognize what it is about the teacher that bugs you.
- Then realize that you are not going to change him or her.
- Finally, ask yourself how you can change your attitude so you can live with the situation.

101

Look again at that teacher. Think about why you can't stand him. Does he seem harsh and rigid, tense and nervous? We forget that teachers have personal lives too. (Hard to believe with some, but it's true!) Something may have happened in his life that makes it a daily struggle for him just to keep going. Try to give him the benefit of the doubt.

Does he remind you of someone you don't like? Personality traits that remind us of someone who has hurt us, ridiculed us, or taken advantage of us can influence our attitudes about a person. Nicole, did you realize we can even hold a grudge against a perfectly nice person for having the same name as someone we do not like? (I don't think you know too many Mickowskis, though!)

Here are some other things that may be coloring your outlook: It may not be the teacher as much as it is the subject. Is it a class you are tolerating only because it is required? What time of day is the class? If it is first period and you don't wake up until third period, this may account for some of the trouble. Any class at the end of the day automatically loses points because you're tired and have had it with school by then. My worst classes were right after lunch—I always wanted to take a siesta!

Face it, Nicole, you may be stuck for the year. How you respond in the situation is what will make the difference. You cannot change the teacher, but you can change your perspective. By now you might have an idea of why you are having the problem.

The next step is to take your eyes off the problem and put them on God. When Peter walked to Jesus on the water, he did just fine until he took his eyes off the Lord and saw the enormous waves and choppy water. Then he began to sink. He cried out, "Lord, save me!" and immediately Jesus reached out his hand and pulled him to safety.

Ask Jesus to help you; then put your trust in him. This is a conscious choice you make. Somewhere in your class note-book put this verse:

Guard my life and rescue me; let me not be put to shame, for I take refuge in you. May integrity and uprightness protect me, because my hope is in you.
PSALM 25:20-21

Nicole, if you want, God can be your bodyguard. Ask him to guard you from harmful words and experiences that may happen at school. Ask God to rescue you from a teacher who may be abusive, or ask God to give you strength to hang in there. God seeks to be our refuge in the storms of life—including those in the classroom.

God can give you protection from teachers who will put you to shame. You know, the ones who make fun of you, put you down, and generally make you think less of yourself. One way that God protects you is through me. If Mr. Mickowski, or any other teacher, starts shaming you or picking on you, let me know. We'll talk about it and figure out some course of action. Sometimes it's just better to transfer out of a class than put up with a lot of unnecessary grief. Wisdom is knowing when to fight and when to walk away.

Learning with you,
Dad

What do you think?

Think of a time when you felt shamed or put down at school. How could God, as your bodyguard, help you in painful times like that?

_____

_____

_____

_____

_____

Pain's Megaphone

TWENTY-SEVEN

God seems to whisper to us in our prosperity but shout at us in our pain.

—DAD

Dear Nicole,

In two seconds your summer was ripped from you. When that woman rear-ended our car, it changed your whole summer. Instead of working at day camp or going to the beach, you have to lie around the house and let your neck heal.

Life isn't fair! If you are like me, you may have asked yourself, *If God is so loving and powerful, why did he let this happen? In fact, why is there so much pain in the world?* Sometimes it feels like God takes the day off. In anger I demand, "Where were you when I needed you?!" Do you ever feel that way?

Nicole, remember when we watched the Persian Gulf War on TV? It was amazing to watch the Scud missiles get destroyed by our Patriot missiles. It was discouraging to see the devastation of the war. I remember thinking, *Why are people so cruel when it comes to war? How could a loving God allow such senseless killing?* Sometimes a loving God doesn't make sense. The world just seems too cruel for a "nice-guy God" to fit in.

The pain in the world is something Christians need to think about. We believe in a loving God who doesn't like suffering and is capable of stopping it, but doesn't. Why not?

God doesn't seem to be doing anything about the starving children, pollution, nuclear threat, and cancer. Could God really stop all the pain and suffering in the world? The answer is yes. And someday he will. But for right now we live in a world of free choice. We have the choice to follow God and his way, or to choose our own course.

According to the Bible (Isaiah 53:6), we all have chosen our own selfish way. God gave us real choices, and we have to live with the real consequences. God could have made us robotic clones who get up in the morning and say, "I love you, God. Plug in my software and I'll do as I am programmed to do." But he didn't.

We were made with free moral choice. That means we have the freedom to decide whether or not we will follow God. It also means that we will have to face the consequences of our decisions (not to mention other people's decisions). Some of the major problems of this world are the leftovers of sinful people making wrong choices.

Nicole, suffering and pain are not God's choice; they are a result of dozens and dozens of choices by sinful people. The good news is that Jesus has the power to overcome all suffering, even death. Jesus himself went through incredible suffering and rejection. He died so our world could be delivered from the mess we got ourselves into.

God is involved in our world and in our pain. He won't wave a magic wand and make pain disappear. But he can deliver us from the trap of sin and the despair of death. With Jesus, we share triumph over those very things that cause pain.

"For I know the plans I have for you," declares the Lord, "plans to prosper you and not to harm you, plans to give you hope and a future. Then you will call upon me and come and pray to me, and I will listen to you."
JEREMIAH 29:11-12

Nicole, it is God's desire to walk with us in our pain and to give us healing. In the midst of our recovery, he'll give us hope and a future. This seems to be the way he works, whether it is physical or emotional pain.

When things are comfortable, easy, and prosperous, I often ignore the gentle whisperings of my heavenly Father. But in the agony and loneliness of pain, I hear his voice as if he's shouting.

It is my prayer for you that in the midst of your pain and discomfort, God would comfort you, heal you, and speak to you, saying, "Nicole, I am healing you because I have an exciting future for you—take hope in that. For I have plans for you—let's talk!"

Hopefully,
Dad

What do you think?

How does God's promise for "hope and a future" help a person in pain?

_____

_____

_____

_____

_____

Enthusiasm Makes the Difference

A mark of a genuine servant is her respect for those who can be of no possible value to her.

—DAD

TWENTY-EIGHT

Dear Nicole,

It gives me great joy to see you teaching your kindergarten class in Children's Celebration. Those kids really like you and look up to you. Even though you were in pain from your neck injury, you studied your lesson, wrote good discussion questions, got up early, and taught your class. That told me a lot. It showed me that you really understand what it means to be a servant. It showed me that you understand responsibility: You had a job to do, and you did it. But probably the strongest quality demonstrated this past Sunday, Nicole, was your compassion for the kids—you love these five-year-olds and it shows!

You are having an impact on these impressionable young children that some of them may never forget. Your enthusiasm helps them feel valued and loved.

Nicole, I was impressed that you wanted to buy a gift for Brian with your own allowance. You showed love with that gift. Remember my definition of love? "Love takes the initiative and acts sacrificially to meet the needs of others." You took the initiative and decided to encourage one of your students. You acted sacrificially by using your own allowance, and you met a real need with that gift. You showed Brian that you love him and think he is special.

It's fun to see you get excited about serving others. It makes life more meaningful, doesn't it? Thanks for taking the time to serve by teaching. As you know, you get more out of it than the kids!

I could tell that this last Sunday was a real test of faith for you. You were in pain, but really wanted to be with your kids. No doubt you asked God to help you. Enthusiasm means being filled with the Spirit of God. It means serving in his power, by his grace. Enthusiasm comes from God's Spirit.

May the God of hope fill you with all joy and peace as you trust in him, so that you may overflow with hope by the power of the Holy Spirit.
ROMANS 15:13

That's what I saw in you, Nicole—an enthusiastic servant! Enthusiasm is the spirit that leads to an effective life. I think you are living an effective, balanced life.

I'm proud of you,
Dad

What do you think?

Why do you think we receive joy when we serve others?

_____

_____

_____

_____

_____

The Passing of Leo

TWENTY-NINE

*Treasure the love you receive above all. It will survive
long after your gold and good health have vanished.*

—OG MANDINO

Dear Nicole,

Remember when Brooke's chameleon died? She didn't seem
too upset to know that Leonardo had gone to the great Lizard
Cage in the Sky. But a few days later, when we were in the car,
Brooke started to cry. Mom didn't know what was wrong, so
she asked.

Brooke cried, "I'm sad because I miss Leo!" She wept in
deep grief for the next twenty minutes.

The interesting thing was that after that we never heard
another comment or saw another tear over Leo the Lizard.

Sometimes grief is like that. You just have to have a time of
sadness before you can go on with life. Life is full of losses. If
it's not lizards, it's cats or dogs or grandmas or divorce. Grief
can hit us in so many ways, and it takes longer for people than
for lizards.

Nicole, as you know, this has been a tough year for me. Two
of my friends died in freak accidents.

I can hardly put on a pair of thongs without thinking of Tim
Pines. Tim always wore his thongs. In a way, thongs symbolized
Tim: casual, comfortable, sensible, and affordable—no expen-
sive dress shoes for this guy! Tim was always the first one to
volunteer to do some lowly job on our youth ministry team.
He didn't really care who got the credit, as long as we understood he was serving as a way to say thanks to God.

Tim always remembered that he was loved by God. It overwhelmed him. I'll never forget staring up at a desert sky filled with stars and hearing Tim say, "To think we are more significant to God than all of those." Nature illustrated for Tim the awesome power of God. It's strange that he should die in a freak avalanche in southern California. I miss Tim. I wish he were here; we could go surfing. Then we could talk about the power of God as seen in the ocean!

I know Tim is in heaven. We'll catch up when I get there.

What will it feel like to be in heaven? Nicole, do you ever wonder? From what the Bible says, heaven is going to feel good! In the first place, when a Christian dies, his body quits working but his soul is "at home with the Lord" (2 Corinthians 5:8). Remember what Jesus told his disciples in John 14?

Do not let your hearts be troubled. Trust in God; trust also in me. In my Father's house are many rooms; . . . I am going there to prepare a place for you. . . . I will come back and take you to be with me.
JOHN 14:1-3

There will be no fear when we die, because the "essence" of us, our real nature, will be with Jesus. Another thing that will happen is that at the time the Bible calls "the last trumpet," all Christians will be given new spiritual bodies (1 Corinthians 15). Whenever the last trumpet call occurs, all believers will be changed "in a flash, in the twinkling of an eye."

I know one of my feelings will be awe. That is bound to be an incredible sight! I will also feel relieved to no longer have my old body, won't you? No more groaning in front of the mirror and trying to make the best of what I've got!

Nicole, another comforting thought is the place God is preparing for us. If God can make an awesome universe in six days, imagine how incredible heaven will be after he's been preparing it for thousands of years—unbelievable!

God is going to do a number on death:

112

*He will swallow up death forever. The Sovereign Lord will wipe
away the tears from all faces; he will remove the disgrace of his
people from all the earth. The Lord has spoken.*

ISAIAH 25:8

We face so many losses on this planet. Death is a tragic loss.
It will be awesome to see God "swallow up death." He is powerful, but he is also personal and caring, for he will "wipe away
the tears from all faces." God loves us so much that he helps us
face the thing we fear most—death. He promises eternal life,
in which we won't be trapped and weighed down with the disgrace of sin. We will be set free to enjoy eternity with the one
who knows us best and loves us most.

Nicole, this helps me as I grieve the loss of my friend Oscar
Diego. He was a faithful coworker on our junior high ministry
team who later became a dearly loved and highly effective
junior high pastor.

It was on one of the junior high events that Oscar drowned
in the lake. He left behind a young wife and an infant son (and
a grieving youth group).

I struggled with God's choice. *Why Oscar? Why not someone
else? Why now?* I really didn't receive answers when I asked these
questions, but I am receiving God's comfort. God reminds me
of the thousands of lives Oscar touched in twenty-nine short
years. He also reminds me of where Oscar is now: playing basketball on the Celestial Courts!

Heaven is incredibly beautiful. There is no darkness or
night. God is the source of light. In heaven we won't be worried or angry, because God is our peace. We will no longer feel
sad, because God will wipe away every tear. We will be very
happy because we will be living exactly according to our
Designer's plan.

Nicole, when I think about where my friends are and what
they are experiencing, it helps me work through the grief. I

imagine that Oscar has met Tim by now, and they are probably doing every adventure and action sport in heaven! Do you think they have bungee jumping in heaven?

Love,

Dad

P.S. Christianity is a great way to live and the only way to die.

What do you think?

What do you think heaven will look like? What do you imagine doing there?

_____

_____

_____

_____

Holy Pride

THIRTY

God is more committed to developing our
character than promoting our comfort.

—DAD

Dear Nicole,

My point in writing you these letters is to give you tools to
make good decisions—decisions you can be proud of, decisions that will help you develop a solid, permanent self-worth.
Our culture tells us that to feel good about ourselves we need
beauty, brains, and bucks. But God's Word offers an approach
that is true, time-tested, and developed by our Creator.

This is what the Lord says: "Let not the wise man boast of his wisdom
or the strong man boast of his strength or the rich man boast of his
riches, but let him who boasts boast about this: that he understands
and knows me, that I am the Lord, who exercises kindness, justice
and righteousness on earth, for in these I delight," declares the Lord.
JEREMIAH 9:23-24

From this Scripture we discover that biblical self-worth
comes from

1. Knowing and understanding God
2. Experiencing God's kindness and grace
3. Experiencing God's forgiveness and justice
4. A growing desire to do the right thing
5. Realizing that these four things delight God

It's so easy to base our self-worth on what *others* think
rather than what *God* thinks.

Nicole, I know you are going through a difficult time with some of your friends. You used to enjoy spending time with Jackie. Now, she has betrayed you. She's even tried to influence Tamara to ignore you. I'm not sure what's going on. I do know that you are hurting. Feeling rejection. Self-confidence shattered.

You have been a caring, giving friend to these girls. Now they stab you in the back.

If you base your self-worth on how these girls treat you—you're in trouble. They have treated you poorly. They have not been considerate or fair.

People will be that way. It hurts. It especially stings if they are people you want to like you—like Jackie and Tamara. But you are valuable, in spite of what they may say or do.

Nicole, trying to score ourselves on how others respond to us is risky business. Somedays they may treat us like heroes. Other days we may be seen as losers. Life is too short to put up with this flakiness. We need to base our self-worth on what *God* thinks, not what *others* think.

There is a lot of pressure to be popular and cool. We all want to be liked. The bottom line is that God is more concerned with your character than your reputation.

Look through the chart on the right to see the difference between reputation and character as foundations for self-worth.

Basing your self-worth on your character is the more accurate and consistent perspective. We will always struggle with self-worth if our goal is to be liked, but we will come to value and accept ourselves as we see ourselves becoming more like Christ.

Nicole, your character is who you are from the inside out. It is where your head meets your heart. I pray that you won't be swept away by the desire to have a reputation of popularity and wind up with fragile self-worth. I hope you will instead continue to pursue Christlike character and not be afraid to stand alone, experiencing God's presence and strength. Then you will truly be *Nicole*—"Victorious Heart"!

Good Reputation	Good Character
Goal: To be liked	Goal: To be like Christ
Focus: What I do	Focus: Who I am
Depends on others' thoughts	Not interested in public opinion
Something you have to strive to earn and achieve	Given to you by God
Exclusive—only for the popular people	Anyone can have it—even people with average reputations
Can be gained or lost quickly	Achieved through a slow process of growth and cannot be taken away
Causes people to play the fool to maintain	Not dependent on success
God may take reputation away to build character	God will not take character away to build a reputation
Afraid of adversity	Survives adversity

My feet have closely followed his steps; I have kept to his way without turning aside.

JOB 23:11

Walking with you,
Dad

What do you think?

Describe a person who is more concerned with becoming popular than with developing character.

_____

_____

_____

_____

_____

Letters to Nicole comes out of my heart—a heart filled with anxiety and love for my daughter. *Anxiety* because I've been working with teens for over twenty years. I know what can happen in adolescence! *Love* because I wanted to help my daughter prepare for, and successfully navigate, adolescence. I don't want to lecture her; I want to equip her.

I knew Nicole could use some positive, personal advice. I also knew it had to be on her terms. Her timetable. Her vocabulary. Her world.

For a year I wrote her these letters. I met her in her world. We walked through life together. Thirty topics. Thirty letters.

I came up with thirty because that seemed to be the length of the books Nicole read. I chose the thirty topics after surveying over five hundred junior high students. These thirty represent their most common questions.

Nicole and I would often discuss these letters, usually on trips—riding in the car, just the two of us.

On our most recent trip together I asked, "What can I do to make this book better? What can we add to make it easier for parents to discuss with their kid?"

"At the end of each letter add just one question. Not a Bible study or a verse. Just one question for the kid to ask their parent, or for the parent to ask their kid."

"Great idea," I said. "What should we call it?"

"How about 'What do you think?'" suggested Nicole. "Make sure you leave room for the kid to write a response if they feel like it."

"Thanks, Nicole. Those are wonderful suggestions."

I set out to rewrite the manuscript and add the "What do you think?" questions. It occured to me that *Letters to Nicole* would primarily be bought by parents as a gift for their daughter or son. I suggest that you read the book before you give it to your child.

As a resource for parents, I have listed all thirty "What do you think?" questions on the next pages. You might want to photocopy them before you give the book to your child. Then you could keep them handy and use them for discussion starters. A few of the questions require reading the chapter first.

Suggestions on how to use the thirty questions

- Go out for breakfast with your child and discuss one or two questions.
- Discuss one question a day for a month.
- Go on a long drive or trip and discuss a few.
- Have an ice-cream date and discuss one.
- Play "one-on-one." Play any game one-on-one (basketball, tennis, chess). Afterwards, over a soft drink, ask your child one of the thirty questions. Then they can ask you a question (it doesn't have to be in the book).
- Invite another family over who has a teen the same age as yours. Write some of the thirty questions on small pieces of paper and place them in a hat. Have parents and children draw and respond to their question.
- Once a month, pick your child up at school and go to a favorite fast food restaurant for lunch. If time is short, take a favorite food to school and meet for lunch. Discuss one of the questions.
- Bedtime story. Tell your child they can stay up an extra fifteen minutes if they talk with you about this important question. Sit on their bed and discuss one question. Tuck them in. (They may like this even if they are seventeen!)
- Use a few of the thirty questions at dinner to stimulate conversations. Choose a few questions and write them on the backs of the napkins. Each person gets to

be the moderator for the question on their own napkin.

- Invite a few parents and their kids to get together for dessert and discussion. Serve dessert, then discuss one to four of the questions. Keep the whole meeting to about an hour or an hour and a half.

These are just some of the ways I have used these questions with teens and parents. Create your own. If you come up with some good ideas, let me know.

After all, we're in this together!

Tim Smith

P.S. To help you in your guided conversation with your child I've written some tips on page 127.

Thirty "What Do You Think?" Discussion Starters

Chapter 1. When did you feel pressure today?

Chapter 2. Besides a roller coaster, what illustration describes your emotions? (Example: "I feel like a dragster, full race—then stop.")

Chapter 3. Complete the following sentence: "I really hate it when . . ."

Chapter 4. What is it about rejection that makes it so scary?

Chapter 5. Why do some people have a difficult time accepting how they look?

Chapter 6. Think of a time when you weren't sure whether you were supposed to act like a kid or an adult. What did you do? How did you feel?

Chapter 7. When is it easy for you to blow things out of proportion and feel defeated?

Chapter 8. What are some good things about feeling shy?

Chapter 9. What has helped you escape temptation?

Chapter 10. Tanya was given a lot of advice. Which piece of advice seems to be the best for you?

Chapter 11. What do you think are some of the benefits and dangers of dating?

Chapter 12. Why do you think God designed rules to go along with his design for sex?

Chapter 13. If God promises "a way out" of sexual temptation, what could be some of those "escape routes"?

Chapter 14. Is it realistic to say something positive about a person instead of gossiping about them?

Chapter 15. If you were given the same assignment as Phil, what would you say is your life philosophy?

Chapter 16. Do you know people like Jimmy, the Party Animal? Do you know someone who could become like Jimmy?

Chapter 17. How does our conscience help us make decisions?

Chapter 18. Do you think music has very much influence on you? Why?

Chapter 19. Think back on a time when you felt close to God. What made you feel that way?

Chapter 20. What is your opinion on teenage drinking? What would you tell your friends if they asked you?

Chapter 21. How does graffiti make you feel? How does it make observers feel? How does it make the owner of the wall feel?

Chapter 22. What do you think about the eight tips for weeding out swearwords? Are they realistic? Helpful? Impossible?

Chapter 23. What do you think about the statement "Where a person allows his feet to take him tells what is important to him"?

Chapter 24. Read that first quote about the three stonecutters. How did their purpose shape their perspective?

Chapter 25. How does God (who is spirit) help us with things that are scary and physical (like earthquakes, fires, and water)?

Chapter 26. Think of a time when you felt shamed or put down at school. How could God, as your bodyguard, help you in painful times like that?

Chapter 27. How does God's promise for "hope and a future" help a person in pain?

Chapter 28. Why do you think we receive joy when we serve others?

Chapter 29. What do you think heaven will look like? What do you imagine doing there?

Chapter 30. Describe a person who is more concerned with becoming popular than with developing character.

Ten Tips on Guided Conversations

1. Love the person more than the question.

2. Be willing to rephrase the question.

3. Be willing to switch to a new topic.

4. Accept each other. Don't force a conversation on someone who is unwilling to have one. Don't belittle or criticize what someone shares.

5. Guided conversations are *guided,* not forced. They are conversations, not monologues.

6. Don't use guided conversations as opportunities to lecture, correct, or suggest.

7. Guided conversations are for sharing, not for teaching (although much learning will take place).

8. Listen to what is being said, but also look for what is being communicated nonverbally.

9. Keep it short. It's better to cut the conversation short and maintain interest than to run it into the ground! By keeping it short, it will be easier to start the next time.

10. Maintain a sense of humor. Don't get too serious. One of the goals is to enjoy each other. Use the conversation to build relationships.

Tim Smith is available for speaking at:
Parent conferences
Dads' workshops
Family camps
Community parenting seminars

For a detailed brochure, write:
WORDSMITH
Tim Smith, Founder
P.O. Box 7736
Thousand Oaks, CA 91359-7736